Anglo-Chinese Encounters since 1
War, Trade, Science and Governanc

M000079990

Chinese encounters with the British were more than merely those between two great powers. There was the larger canvas of the Empire and Commonwealth where the two peoples traded and interacted. In China, officials and merchants placed the British beside other enterprising foreign peoples who were equally intent on influencing developments there. There were also Chinese who encountered the British in personal ways, and individual British who ventured into a "vast unknown" with its deep history. Wang Gungwu's book, based on lectures linking China and the Chinese with imperial Britain, examines the possibilities, as well as the limitations, attached to their encounters. It takes the story beyond the clichés of opium, fighting, and the diplomatic skills needed to fend off rivals and enemies, and probes some areas of more intimate encounters, not least the beginnings of a wider English-speaking future between the two countries.

Wang Gungwu is Professor and Director, East Asian Institute, National University of Singapore. His publications include *Bind Us in Time: Nation and Civilisation in Asia* (2002) and *To Act is to Know: Chinese Dilemmas* (2002).

Anglo-Chinese Encounters since 1800
War, Trade, Science and Governance

WANG GUNGWU
National University of Singapore

PUBLISHED BY THE PRESS SYNDICATE OF THE UNIVERSITY OF CAMBRIDGE
The Pitt Building, Trumpington Street, Cambridge, United Kingdom

CAMBRIDGE UNIVERSITY PRESS
The Edinburgh Building, Cambridge, CB2 2RU, UK
40 West 20th Street, New York, NY 10011-4211, USA
477 Williamstown Road, Port Melbourne, VIC 3207, Australia
Ruiz de Alarcón 13, 28014 Madrid, Spain
Dock House, The Waterfront, Cape Town 8001, South Africa

http://www.cambridge.org

First published 2003

Printed in China through Bookbuilders

Typefaces Bembo 12.75/15 pt   *System* LATEX 2$_\varepsilon$ [TB]

A catalogue record for this book is available from the British Library

National Library of Australia Cataloguing in Publication data
Wang, Gungwu, 1930–.
Anglo-Chinese encounters since 1800: war, trade, science and governance.
Bibliography.
Includes index.
ISBN 0 521 82639 X.
ISBN 0 521 53413 5 (pbk.).
1. China – Foreign relations – Great Britain. 2. Great
Britain – Foreign relations – China. 3. China – Commerce –
Great Britain. 4. Great Britain – Commerce – China. I. Title.
327.51041

ISBN 0 521 82639 X hardback
ISBN 0 521 53413 5 paperback

To my grandchildren

Sebastian WANG Lisheng
Katharine Yisheng REGAN
Ryan WANG Kaisheng
Samantha Feisheng REGAN

Contents

Acknowledgments

I am grateful to the Smuts Memorial Fund for the invitation in 1995 to give the Commonwealth Lectures at the University of Cambridge in 1996–1997. A couple of months before I was supposed to give these lectures, unforeseen circumstances forced me to cancel my trip altogether. This caused great inconvenience to the organisers, and especially to my host, Gordon Johnson, President of Wolfson College, Cambridge.

In preparation for the lectures, I sketched out the story of Anglo-Chinese encounters, in China, in Britain and in the Commonwealth. I had just spent nearly ten years working on the edge of China in the last major British colony of Hong Kong, and recently translated to Singapore, a member state of the Commonwealth that was already over thirty years old. The two island port cities seemed to be good starting points from which I could make my excursions. I have never strictly observed modern political boundaries in my readings of modern Chinese history. As someone who was born Chinese in a Dutch colony, Java in the Netherlands East Indies, but has lived all but three years of my life in countries that are, or were, parts of the British Empire and Commonwealth, I had often wondered if I could bring the Chinese and British stories together in some way. The Smuts Commonwealth Lectures would make an interesting framework for me to reflect on some of the encounters the two peoples have had since 1800.

It came as a pleasant surprise two years later when the Smuts Memorial Fund renewed its invitation to give the Commonwealth Lectures in the year 2000. Again, Gordon Johnson offered to be host. This was a generous gesture and gave me an opportunity to return to the notes and sketches I had made. This volume is a slightly revised version of the lectures I gave in Cambridge in October 2000.

1 Introduction

It is a great honour for me to be invited to give the Smuts Commonwealth Lectures. I grew up in Ipoh in the state of Perak, a British protected state, and studied Empire and Commonwealth history for my Cambridge School Certificate in a government-funded school named after Governor Sir John Anderson (1858–1918). Jan Christiaan Smuts (1870–1950) was still alive when I went to university in Singapore, in the newly established University of Malaya. I was interested in the extraordinary story of how this Cambridge-educated colonial became first a bitter foe of the British Empire and then a loyal supporter of the Commonwealth. This interest was fuelled by my meeting Keith Hancock (1898–1988) at the Australian National University in 1968 when he had just completed the second volume of his biography of Smuts.[1] I enjoyed reading about the young Boer's youth and his exploits in the War of 1899–1902. The last stage of his career after 1933 intrigued me even more. Why did he become so loyal to the Commonwealth? Among the reasons that might be offered for this loyalty, two stood out for me as a Chinese sojourner. One was that he was of European descent, a Christian, someone who could identify with British culture and history, and who also trained to be a common law lawyer in one of the great universities in the world. The other was that he was a settler colonist with a deep love of the land of his ancestors in South Africa and he wanted his people to build their own civilised country in a multiracial continent. Thus, he worked to perpetuate the Commonwealth as an institution that would enable his country to become free and humane and a part of a global enterprise.

Neither explanation applied to my life, however, and this was the reason why I did not embark on research in Commonwealth history when I had the chance to do so. I was born to parents from literati families who had served the Chinese imperial system. But the 1911 revolution in China changed the lives of such families. My father switched from studying the traditional Confucian classics to prepare to enter a modern university. After he graduated, he found that he had to leave China to find the kind of work he wanted and started his teaching life as a sojourner in British Malaya.[2] He then went home to marry my mother and they both went to the Netherlands East Indies. I was born in Surabaya where my father was a Chinese high school principal. He left Java to go to the Malay State of Perak when I was a small child, and took a job with the Education Department under British administration as an inspector of Chinese schools. Although my father had studied English at university in China and was a great admirer of English literature, he never brought me up to identify with the British Empire. However, his work introduced him to certain imperial ways of dealing with a plural society. He thus saw his task as ensuring that Chinese children had a good modern education and that the Chinese community did their bit to transmit Chinese culture to those who wanted it. My mother knew Chinese well but did not speak or understand any English, so we spoke only Chinese at home. For them both, Malaya was not really their home and they had no deeper wish than to return to their homeland in China. They also imparted to their only child a love for China and things Chinese.[3]

So why do I think I have something to say about the Commonwealth? One of my qualifications comes from the fact that I have lived all but three years of my life in countries that were once part of the Empire or are still members of the Commonwealth. Those years were spent in various towns and cities of Malaya and Malaysia, in the United Kingdom, in Australia, in Hong Kong, and finally in independent Singapore. The other qualification is more mixed. I learnt my history at university from British teachers and colleagues[4] even though I have spent most of my professional life writing about the history of China and the Chinese overseas. I did my research, teaching and writing in Commonwealth-type universities and environments[5] and this has given me ample opportunities to reflect on the Anglo-Chinese connection, both within and outside the Commonwealth. Thus, I have often wondered about how various kinds of Chinese have fared in their dealings with the British and what China has made of the encounters with various British and their activities in Asia.

These lectures therefore have been written from that perspective. They do not attempt to be comprehensive about all aspects of British relations with China and the Chinese, but come at the subject from both the Chinese and British periphery and seek to juxtapose issues that were central to the two peoples with those that might seem to be tangential. My use of the word "encounter" does not have the qualities described by Gillian Beer of being "forceful, dangerous, alluring, essential", but I hope, as she suggests, "it brings into active play unexamined assumptions and so may allow interpreters, if not always the principals, to tap into unexpressed incentives".[6] The angle of vision I have chosen is sometimes awkward, and the picture presented is elusive and hardly ever the whole story. The key to the story, however, is that, on the most serious matters pertaining to their deeply felt values, both the British and the Chinese people remained far apart.

My story begins with the theme that the British and the Chinese had a turbulent relationship from the start. There was never enough that was right between them to enable either to develop a deeper understanding of the other. There were complex reasons for this. Some arose from immediate political and economic conflicts, but most of them stemmed from deep differences in history and culture. There should be nothing surprising in that. The Western civilisation that had nourished the British nation was very different from the unique civilisation that China had produced for itself. Also, the British had had to deal with other great civilisations before they first met the Chinese. In fact, the British had a great deal more to do with the two civilisations of the Muslims and the Hindus in West and South Asia than with the Chinese, and they did not get much right with them either. The British, in accumulating imperial territories, were always outnumbered. Sensing that their power would always be insecure, they erected protective barriers that were extended to cover social and cultural relationships. Not enough of them could afford to lower their defences when faced with the alien and the bewildering.

Nevertheless, the Anglo-Chinese relationship was a rich and productive one. Although so different, the English- and Chinese-speaking worlds came tantalisingly close on many occasions and indeed there were some encounters that have had profound effects on China. For example, the Chinese felt the sting of British naval power but admired more the fact that that power came from a modern sovereign nation-state. Their re-assessments of the defence and security of their country have been continuous, but the transformation that the country needed to respond to that kind of power was late in coming. Also, the Chinese official classes were struck by the wealth that overseas commercial enterprises could produce. This eventually prepared them to review the status of Chinese merchants and seek to redefine the roles that these merchants could play in China's recovery. Furthermore, different groups of Chinese responded to a British missionary culture in very different ways but, in the end, it was British technological advances that won the most converts. As a result, the idea of science has become the measure of modern civilisation and now determines the meaning of modern education for all China's peoples. Finally, most Chinese were struck by British respect for the law, their civic discipline and efficiency, even though they did not always appreciate how that respect was cultivated. Nor has it been easy to understand the ramifications of a system of governance based on the rule of law. But there is no doubt that the cumulative impact of a wide range of encounters has been profound.

I shall explore some of these past encounters and reflect on their present and future significance. Chapters two and three will focus on Chinese attitudes towards war and the strategies of entrepreneurs overseas. These will be followed by two other chapters on the rediscovery of China's scientific past and the Chinese response to modern statecraft, including their experiments with political parties. I shall then try to draw these thoughts together to offer a long view of the Anglo-Chinese phenomenon.

When thinking about the Anglo impact on China as compared with that on India, I was struck to read the following lines by the nineteenth-century Indian Muslim poet Mirza Ghalib (1797–1869)[7] when he advised Sayyid Ahmad Khan (1817–1898), the founder of the Aligarh Muslim University in India, not to look so much to the Mughal past. The lines were:

> Open thine eyes, and examine the Englishmen,
> Their style, their manner, their trade and their art.[8]

This would not have been advice that the Chinese mandarins of the time would have heeded and there were important cultural reasons why that was so. It is also a measure of the different starting points in Indian (both Hindu and Muslim) and Chinese worldviews. Of the four qualities Ghalib wanted Sayyid Ahmad Khan to examine, only "their trade" might have attracted the Chinese merchants on the coast, but that was precisely what the mandarin rulers had set out to limit and control. In no way would they have encouraged Chinese merchants to learn from English trading ways. And that would have been even more true of "their manner" and "their style" which, on the whole, the mandarins found reason actively to dislike. Some Chinese might have found "their art" interesting, especially in its use in design and industrial arts, and also the inventiveness in the use of materials but, most of the time, the Chinese would have been more impressed by what made the British powerful.

What, then, would have focused the Chinese mind? I have found that Arthur Waley (1889–1966) captured that best in a piece he wrote in 1942, in the middle of the Second World War, called "A Debt to China". It was reprinted two years later in Hsiao Ch'ien's (1910–1999) *A Harp with a Thousand Strings*.[9] Waley spoke of "a great turning-point in our relations with China" during the first two decades of the twentieth century when men of leisure, poets, professors, thinkers, began to visit China instead of the usual soldiers, sailors, missionaries, merchant and officials. It seems somewhat surprising that he should have drawn attention to this. As Ivan Morris put it,

> The strangest thing about Waley was his failure to visit China and Japan. I asked him about this, but never received a direct answer. Raymond Mortimer is surely right when he says that Waley 'felt so much at home in T'ang China and Heian Japan that he could not face the modern ugliness amid which one has to seek out the many intact remains of beauty'. He carried his own images of China and Japan within himself and had no wish to dilute them by tourism.[10]

Nevertheless, he was part of the "great turning point" in demystifying Chinese poetry for the English-speaking world and walked his own path towards a deep mental and aesthetic encounter with the Chinese. It was a pity, however, that so few Chinese were aware how that sensibility could work its verbal magic on Chinese ideas, language and art.

In his essay, Arthur Waley went on to mention a few men who went "not to convert, trade, rule or fight,

but simply to make friends and learn". He thought
such visitors would have given the Chinese a completely new view of the British. Of the men he mentioned, Goldsworthy Lowes Dickinson (1862–1932) and
Robert Trevelyan (1872–1951) made no impact. Only
Bertrand Russell (1872–1970) left an impression, but
men like him were too few and most of them had gone
to China too late to make many friends. In reality, his
earlier four words, "to convert, trade, rule or fight", remained truer than he might have wished. He cannot, of
course, be blamed for not foreseeing that Britain was to
be succeeded by an even more powerful force to which
the same four words could apply. I refer to the informal
empire of the United States that, perhaps unwittingly, has
replaced the British Empire not only in the eyes of the
Chinese but also of other peoples living in the regions of
East and Southeast Asia. Informally or not, the United
States' accession to a second phase of Anglo-Chinese
encounter has made the larger picture seem continuous
and seamless to the present day. I therefore suggest that
Waley's four words remain central to that extended story.
The words, "convert, trade, rule or fight", describe the
core issues in the history of Chinese relations with the
English-speaking peoples.

I shall not, however, follow Waley's word order but
begin with "to fight", the word that captured China's
full attention as none of the other three did. China's first
humiliating defeat by Britain in 1842 was an ill-fated
start, and was probably why the two peoples never did
quite get anything right between them thereafter. The
next would be "to trade", something that had begun
much earlier but whose full impact did not come until
after all the fighting was done. Here the Chinese had

a much better measure of the British and their mutual assessments of each other, as they widened their common enterprises over time, were usually more right than wrong. As for "to convert", this was rather one-sided. The Chinese tradition paid little attention to converting others, but when the word was stretched to include both sacred and secular education, this was a fertile area for mutual exploration. It turned out in the end to be one where nothing was ever quite right, but the Chinese did manage to take much of only what they wanted from the contact. Finally, "to rule" was even more one-sided but this was necessarily a partial, if not peripheral, experience for most Chinese. After having to rule India before opening up the coast of China, the British did not relish the idea of ruling over China. But rule they did over bits of administration, whether in the Treaty Ports or in the maritime customs, and over Chinese communities outside China, notably in Hong Kong, Malaya and parts of north Borneo. Here the response of the Chinese was mixed indeed, but the potential for a deeper understanding of the essential features of modern governance was often there and deserves attention.

As I shall be talking a lot about China, I shall obviously be neglecting issues closer to the Commonwealth for which the Smuts Memorial Lectures have been named. I hope you will bear with me when I suggest that, the motives of the politicians who created it notwithstanding, the ideals underlying the Commonwealth go beyond those of a cozy club consisting of member countries that have shared a common past. They were drawn from ideals which represented a bold attempt to generalise some unique experiences of a multicultural and multiracial world, and to make enough order out of those

experiences for others to study if not emulate. China itself was not directly part of that world and will still insist
on its own vision in order that it might yet play an important role in defining the future of that world. But there
are now millions of Chinese outside China who are living with various social and economic systems, a major
part of them in an extension of the English-speaking empire now informally led by the United States. They are
now useful links between China and a globalised world.

Jan Christiaan Smuts would have understood the
changes in perspective between the first half of the twentieth century and the second. He was the most internationalist Boer of his generation. He admired Winston
Churchill's worldview, regretted American isolationism,
feared the rise of Soviet Russia, and recognised the in-
evitability of Indian independence. He wrote on China,
with foreboding, in September 1937, following the outbreak of war with Japan,

> What will the giant yet do when fully released? I fear Japan
> has done a thing which may not only undo her yet, but which
> may threaten the West far more in the coming generations
> than anything that has happened in the East in the past. The
> heroism of the Chinese may yet shake the world.[11]

His tragedy was, in his own words, the "fear of getting
submerged in black Africa...What can one do about
it, when the Lord himself made the mistake of creating colour!"[12] Thus he did not blame the British for
not getting it right about South Africa. In retrospect,
the British were wrong to have fought the Boers. Also,
they fought badly even though they eventually won
the war. In the end, they failed to stop the creation

of one of the nastiest regimes in the Commonwealth. But they did get it right with trade, with economic development, and South Africa did become the richest country in the continent. As for "converting" some people to Christian ideals, some credit must go to the Anglo-Christian world for someone like Nelson Mandela to be possible. Mandela could be compared, as in the Chinese saying, to the fresh and beautiful lotus flowers and leaves that grow out of the mud but are totally free of mud. Such a flowering is something the Chinese literati-mandarins would have deeply admired.

What is more, there is yet another extraordinary, if inadvertent, product of the empire in that region. I refer to the great nationalist leader of India, Mahatma Gandhi (1867–1948), who had worked as a lawyer in South Africa and was a contemporary of Smuts. Gandhi would have rejected all four of the words Arthur Waley used for the British in China if they had been applied to India: fighting, trading, converting and ruling. He rejected all fighting because there had simply been too much killing in India by both Indians and British, and he saw no way of winning his particular war on the battlefield. He also rejected Christianity as a church, although appreciating its spiritual power. He openly referred to those parts of Christian beliefs that could help him revivify his own faith. Even more vehemently, he rejected British rule, and his non-violent solutions to each problem he met with on the road to independence baffled even the hard-headed British empire-builders. Lastly, he rejected the kind of trading in mass-produced manufactures that gave the British their dominance in Indian markets and undermined the traditional economy and culture of the Indian peasantry.

On all four counts of rejection, no Chinese political leader was as thorough and unbending as Mahatma Gandhi. The Chinese leaders who preached thorough reform and revolution, like Kang Youwei (1858–1927) and Sun Yat-sen (1866–1925), and fierce nationalists like Chiang Kai-shek (1887–1975), and Mao Zedong (1893–1976) when young, had all been more responsive than Gandhi was to the modern and the secular that the British were seen to represent. Like most pragmatic Chinese, they were willing to learn, albeit not from Britain specifically, but from the models of Western Europe. Why, then, does it appear today that Anglo-Indian encounters have borne more fruit than Anglo-Chinese ones, or more than has been produced by the impact on China of the West as a whole? I shall not try to answer that question, but hope that what I say about Anglo-Chinese encounters here can help others to tackle what appears to be an intriguing puzzle.

2 "To fight"

Let me start with one of Arthur Waley's words, "to fight". The British opening of China in the 1840s was the result of their success in breaking through Chinese naval and coastal defences and the trauma of that defeat for Chinese leaders lasted for generations. It became the most important marker for Chinese historiography when this "Opium War" was chosen, soon after the fall of the Qing dynasty in 1911, to date the beginnings of China's modern history. That decision reflects both a new reality and China's strong desire not to forget the aftermath of regret, resentment and recrimination. The subject has filled hundreds of volumes in a number of languages. The actual fighting has also been fully described many times and the details need not detain us. It is enough to focus here on some of the consequences for China.

The British had conquered much territory in India but did not try to do the same in China. They had fought the Indians for far longer a period, at least 100 years from the Battle of Plassey to the Mutiny, and thereafter against local insurrections and the enemies who threatened the Northwest Frontier. But they did not have to fight long with the Chinese, mainly from 1840 to 1860, because they started fighting the Chinese only after they had

already become the strongest power in the world and the
Chinese empire was in decline. The British soon had
all that they wanted. In addition, the British had many
competitors who were willing to share or do more of
the fighting whenever they thought that it was in their
interests: for example, the French and the Russians, and
later the Germans and the Japanese. If anything, it soon
became clear that what was increasingly important for
Britain was to help the Chinese modernise themselves
in military affairs. The British wanted trade, not land. If
Chinese armies could keep order in their own land, trade
would prosper. There was, in any case, no question of the
Chinese ever becoming a military threat to the British
themselves. All that was needed was for the British navy
to patrol the Yangzi river regularly and remain in a
state of armed readiness in bases like Hong Kong and
Singapore.

The British did teach the Chinese ruling elites their
most important lesson. This was that the Chinese realm
could be seriously threatened from the south and from
the east, and that it could even be conquered from the
sea. The Chinese rulers had not been ready to learn
that lesson when they first saw European ships fighting off their coasts from the sixteenth to the eighteenth centuries. It was also not a lesson that they learnt
willingly. What they had been aware of for centuries
was that they could build a strong naval force if they
wanted to (at least since the Song dynasty, 960–1276).[1]
During the first half of the fifteenth century, the third
emperor of the Ming dynasty (1368–1644), Emperor
Yongle (1402–1424), could, and did, send naval expeditions through Southeast Asia and across the Indian
Ocean to the coasts of Arabia and eastern Africa. He

and his successors had the capacity to defeat Japanese and other pirates and armed traders who disturbed the peace of coastal towns and cities. During the middle of the sixteenth century, after 120 years of neglect, it was still possible to rebuild a navy strong enough to defend the empire against Japanese and Chinese pirates. By the beginning of the seventeenth century, Chinese armed merchants, especially those led by Zheng Chenggong (1624–1662), better known to the maritime world at the time as Koxinga, had established one of the strongest navies in the region to control the trade between Japan, the Chinese coast and Southeast Asia.[2]

But the Manchu Qing dynasty (1644–1911) reorganised the imperial navy and ultimately destroyed Koxinga's base in Taiwan in 1684. After that victory, the Manchu court devised a tight system of deprivation and control of all foreign trade in order to ensure that the empire would never have to deal with such mercantile enemies again. This proved to be a successful policy for more than 100 years, until the early nineteenth century. The Manchus were simply not aware that, while their military forces were complacent and stagnating with their older fighting methods, their future enemies were advancing fast in the skills of warfare.

For the Chinese empire throughout its history, defence of its northern land borders was most important. The Ming rulers turned away from the sea after the first third of the fifteenth century precisely for that reason when they found their Mongol enemies once again at their gates. The Manchus, themselves overland conquerors of the Chinese heartland, were even more sensitive to what could happen if the northern frontiers were weak. They read Chinese history carefully and

concluded that there were no enemies who could have
conquered China from the sea. Even after Lord Macartney's visit in 1793, with the ambassador's open display of
pride and confidence, Qing coastal officials still did not
report accurately to Emperor Qianlong the intelligence
already available about British naval prowess.[3] Not until
the British ships fought their way up the Pearl River to
Canton (Guangzhou) in 1841 did the Qing court first
realise China's relative weakness.

Most nationalist historians in China during the twentieth century have castigated the Manchu court for its
failure to prepare China for war against the British.
Much of their historical writing has also concentrated
on the corrupt and treacherous officials who either mis-
led the emperor or underestimated the enemy. The only
praise for the higher officials has been reserved for Commissioner Lin Zexu (1785–1850) for having defied the
British and confiscated British opium. At lower levels of
the Qing armed forces, there has been appreciation of
some of the military officers who bravely defended the
poorly designed coastal forts. But the warmest accolades
have gone to the people of villages like Sanyuanli outside
Guangzhou who had stood up to British troops. All this
was hardly noticed then, and only came to be recognised
afterwards, when nationalist historians went to work.[4] At
the time, early in the 1840s, the Qing court had little
time to assess the damage along the coast when it was
engaged in the desperate struggles with local rebellions
in the interior. By 1851, these too were overshadowed
by the greatest threat to the empire since the seventeenth
century, the Taiping Heavenly Kingdom, whose armies
swept through south and central China and made its
capital in the empire's second capital in Nanjing. This

was followed by several other rebellions in the north, northwest and southwest, wars that engaged the imperial armies for the next thirty years.[5]

In the eyes of the court, the empire managed, not surprisingly, to win all these land battles. The British in Shanghai did provide timely help to fight off the Taiping armies in the neighbouring counties of the Yangzi delta area at the time when these rebels were at their most dangerous. But the imperial forces that did the key fighting were built around the loyal Chinese militia units (called the "Hunan braves") brought together by the scholar official, Zeng Guofan (1811–1872), and the local gentry leaders whom he had inspired. These armies fought against the Nian rebels in the north and the major Muslim rebellions in Yunnan (on the Burma border) and Xinjiang (Chinese Turkestan), and eventually defeated them all.[6] Thus, despite the fact that Qing officials could not prevent further debacles in Anglo-Chinese relations in the 1850s and their troops failed to prevent British and French naval forces from taking Beijing and sacking the Summer Palace, they could still interpret those disasters as merely partial setbacks, and remained hopeful that these would be temporary. The contrast between relative success on land and painful performance at sea did not seem to have been so obvious.

Wei Yuan (1794–1856), the author of *Haiguo tuzhi* (Illustrated Records of the Maritime Countries, published in 1844), the earliest and best available study of China's maritime position at the end of that war, concluded that, if China was ever to defend itself against its enemies again, the court would have to learn Western naval technology and use Western skills to train Chinese sailors.[7] But the message was read as a general warning and not taken seriously for another two decades. Indeed, a thorough examination of what the Chinese side knew of the relative strengths of the British and Qing military before the outbreak of the Opium War was not done even during the late Qing dynasty. Long after the fall of the dynasty, in the 1930s and the 1940s, several historians examined British archival records and provided rich details about China's weaknesses in defence, including its lack of a modern navy. But what was missing was the realisation by both Qing and Republican political leaders that there had been throughout the nineteenth century a fundamental gap in understanding about the nature of seapower. That lack lasted for more than a century.

In post-1949 historiography, there have been numerous studies of the Opium War and the patriotism of Commissioner Lin Zexu.[8] Lin Zexu's many admiring biographies all touch on his mistakes but focus on his attempts to learn about the potential enemy before deciding to fight, and also on his courage and the dilemmas he faced. There have been efforts to find those literati who did realise the dangers that China faced but whose advice had fallen on deaf ears. There have also been writings that depicted the heroism of ordinary Chinese in Guangdong and outside Shanghai who fought the British in vain. But it has fallen to Mao Haijian of the Academy of Social Science in Beijing in his book, *Tianchao de bengkui* (The Collapse of the Heavenly Dynasty), published in 1995, to reach the more specific but unpopular conclusion that the Chinese mandarins of that generation, including Commissioner Lin himself, had not done enough homework, either about coastal defences and naval warfare, or about the firepower of the British forces. They had simply underestimated the

British. Otherwise, they would have known that China was in no position to challenge Britain and would not have been so ready to provoke the Opium War before adequate preparations had been made. The real lesson was not about bravery, or patriotism, or even technology, but about a complete reappraisal of what it would have taken to create the necessary defence for the empire, the kind of rethinking that would have included new attitudes towards the navy. It is particularly noteworthy that Mao Haijian's book has the most complete study of all the British warships operating in China waters in the 1840s, more so than any previous Chinese work on this period.[9]

In the 1860s, however, "to fight" for the Chinese meant desperate defence against enemies from all directions while, for the British, it was more a question of *not* fighting the Chinese again, but helping the Chinese keep internal law and order so that they could fight other enemies for themselves. The Qing court engaged a number of British advisers to equip and train their Bannerman battalions in modern weaponry, but these largely addressed the modernisation of land forces. Mandarin soldiers like Zeng Guofan had become aware that the lack of naval power was a serious deficiency in the imperial defences. He and his most innovative subordinates soon made plans to build a modern navy and sought British help to repair that weakness.

The views of Zuo Zongtang (1812–1885), one of the great generals of the period of Qing "restoration" after the Taiping rebellion, reflect well the ambivalence about what had to be done. On the one hand, he strongly recommended the establishment of a great shipyard, a modern arsenal, and a training academy for the navy.

On the other, he had to fight a brutal and successful land war in the northwestern region of Xinjiang
against Muslim rebels and sought loans for that war
at the expense of naval development. He justified this
with the argument that China's land enemies sought
territory with the backing of either Tsarist Russia or
British India, while its naval enemies merely sought trading privileges. In fairness to Zuo Zongtang, the Qing
court was never committed to developing a strong navy
anyway, despite the fine start given to its creation by
Shen Baozhen (1820–1879) in Fuzhou (Foochow) between 1867–1874. It is also interesting that Zuo Zongtang was unhappy that the British, who were supposed
to help, had not been more forthcoming. He noted that
Sir Robert Hart (1835–1911) asked only to build a merchant fleet while Sir Thomas Wade (1818–1895) spoke
vaguely of training naval personnel.[10] It led him to distrust British advice and ask French naval officials instead
to help with the shipbuilding facilities.

Shen Baozhen, on the other hand, realised that it
was the British who knew most about navigation and
engaged British naval officers from the Royal Naval
College at Greenwich to help train the early batches
of students at the Fuzhou Navy Yard. Later, he was also
shrewd enough to send some of his brightest students to
England. He was well aware that the Japanese had also
turned to the British for naval training and shipbuilding.
Although the mixture of French and British staff at the
Navy Yard was, in the end, a mistake, a contemporary
British observer of the Yard's development over a period of twenty years commented that "In Foochow you
had a very good naval college. You want four colleges
like that of Foochow". By then, in 1884, the Foochow

squadron itself was about to be wiped out by the French. Nevertheless, it has been concluded that "The School itself became a model institution in China... When Li Hung-Chang founded the naval academy at Tientsin and established the Peiyang fleet, he relied heavily on Foochow-trained men."[11] But, by that time, there were not only rival centres of naval training, but also rival offers of help from German and American interests in addition to the earlier French offers. Deep-seated unease about relying too much on the British contributed to undermining efforts to bring naval development under a unified control.[12]

One of the fascinating questions in East Asia later in the century was that concerning the fighting between the two sets of students trained by the British – which of them would learn better? On the eve of the Sino-Japanese War in 1894, there were nominally four naval squadrons in China: the Beiyang force in the north, the Nanyang along the coast south of Shandong, and the two provincial ones for Fujian and Guangdong, with nearly 100 naval vessels of various sizes, totaling 80,000 tons. The main force was the Beiyang squadron when war broke out with Japan in 1894. Within a few weeks, the question was answered. When the Japanese engaged the Chinese in the decisive naval battles off the coast of Shandong and the Liaodong peninsula, the active Chinese fleet was wiped out.[13]

What went wrong with the naval shipyards and the training? Yan Fu (1854–1921), trained in Foochow Navy Yard and for many years the head of the Beiyang Naval Academy, has suggested an answer. This was found in the words of Sir Robert Hart in the 1880s that he recalled in 1918. He quotes Hart as having said:

A navy is to a country what flowers are to a tree. Only when
the roots and branches are flourishing, and wind and sun,
water and soil are agreeable, will the flowers blossom. The
flowers produce fruit and this ensures that the tree will grow
strong with age. There are many problems about your country's navy that are unsatisfactory, but they can only be tackled
by going back and examining the roots. It will be useless to
seek the solutions only within the navy itself.[14]

It is often forgotten, even by the Chinese themselves,
that the Chinese did once have the most powerful navy
in the world and had the skills to build great ocean-going
warships that could take the offensive. Chinese historians
are wont to blame the failures of 1894–1895 on the ex-
travagance of the Empress Dowager (Empress Xiaoqin,
commonly known as Cixi, 1835–1908), who failed to
provide enough funding for the navy. Even if this were
the sole explanation for failure, it is stark confirmation
of the Qing court's inability to adjust to the new world
of naval power. In fact, there had been sustained neglect
of naval forces for more than four centuries, and there
was certainly no sense of priority about the need for a
modern fighting force at sea.

The British continued to assist with naval planning
and reorganisation, and the Chinese imperial fleet did
recover enough after 1900 to show its colours across the
Pacific, Indian and Atlantic oceans. But, by that time,
there was no pretence that the fleet was any match for
the great navies of Britain, Japan and the United States,
nor much more than one that was primarily for river
and coastal patrols. When the Boxer Rebellion of 1900
provoked an international force to be sent to lift the siege
of the legations in Peking, there followed a number of

clear demonstrations of the Qing empire's inability to fight at all. Not only was there no navy to speak of, but the armies also offered little resistance. It could not have escaped the court's attention that there were Chinese overseas living in Western colonies who donated funds to support the forces sent to relieve the foreign legations. Clearly, these no longer identified with the Qing dynasty and shared the growing consensus in the West that Chinese civilisation was decadent and irretrievably in decline.[15]

So desperate were China's leaders that, after 1900, they sent their officers to be trained in Japan, the erstwhile enemy they had once despised. Why the Japanese? Ever since the 1860s, many British and American scholars, including missionaries who knew the Chinese language, had helped to translate a large number of scientific, geographical, military, political and legal writings for the use of mandarins, officers and their technical staff, as well as prepare students to be sent for further education and training in Europe and the United States. Unfortunately, it was thought enough to master a few key texts. Once these were available for study, that served the purpose of the mandarins. Why was the updating of such texts taken less seriously and systematic translation of new works not followed up? The reasons for this are complex. I shall come to this in chapter four when questions of conversion and education are dealt with. Here I shall concentrate on the more immediate advantages of turning to Japan rather than to Britain in order to learn how to fight modern wars.

To begin with, Japan was much nearer and it cost much less for the Chinese to study there. Most of all, the Japanese had already themselves translated all the important military books and technical manuals they needed. It was clear that they had been very successful there, something which the Chinese could do well to emulate. But, instead of starting afresh, it was much easier for Chinese to master the Japanese written language than to learn other foreign languages, and it would save time and money to have these works translated into Chinese from the Japanese. Indeed, the evidence of the rapid availability of Western books and essays in Chinese, including books on modern warfare, before the end of the first decade of the twentieth century, is overwhelming.[16] In addition, it was thought that there would be greater cultural empathy from the Japanese. This is understandable. But that this also included the illusion of sharing goals of imperial restoration against the common Western enemy, including Tsarist Russia and an expansionist Germany, all waiting to carve China into little colonial pieces, showed how desperate the Qing officials had become. In any case, they noted that British imperial interests had led the British to cultivate friendlier relations with Japan, and that this had contributed to Japan's great naval victories against the Russian Far Eastern Fleet in 1904–1905. This confirmed to the Chinese that they gained little by depending on advisers from an over-extended British Empire but could learn much more from their near neighbour.

The 1911 revolution that overthrew the Manchus could have offered a fresh start in rethinking military priorities. The influence of foreign military training on many of the key protagonists on both sides of the war is well known. There were the graduates of the Beiyang Military Academy who had studied with British and other Western military officers and advisers. And there

were those who were specially recruited after training in
Japan to establish units of the New Army for Yuan Shikai
(1859–1916), the first President and chief beneficiary of
this minor military renaissance. Yet others had been sent
by Zhang Zhidong (1837–1909) when he was Viceroy
at Huguang (Hubei and Hunan provinces in Central
China) to study in Japan and form the core of the New
Army in Central China. When the revolution broke out
in the Wuhan area on 10 October 1911, both sides were
led by young officers who had been fellow students in
Japanese military academies. And when the revolutionary cause was lost to the militarists under Yuan Shikai,
again the younger officers on both sides of the political
conflicts that ensued had links with Japan. For example,
Li Yuanhong (1864–1928), the former naval officer who
gave up his career after the defeat by Japan to become
eventually the senior local commander in Wuhan, and
unwillingly the head of revolutionary forces in 1911,
had made several visits to Japan while training the New
Army. Indeed, for another decade and a half afterwards,
during the period of division called the "Warlord period", many of the most senior officers who served the
warlords had had spells of training in Japan.[17]

Thus the period 1901–1914 marked a turning
point for Anglo-Chinese military relations. Thereafter,
the British impact on China's military reorganisation
and recovery was negligible. During the struggles for
supremacy among the warlords after Yuan Shikai's death
in 1916, another fact stood out. The battles did not in-
volve any naval forces and there was no money to build
a navy anyway. The challengers for national leadership
were warlords who understood land forces, men like
Wu Peifu (1874–1939), Zhang Zuolin (1873–1928), and

Feng Yuxiang (1882–1948), men who never needed to think about the navy. Indeed, there was no urgent need to spend money or energy to do so because the age of naval threats to the country was over. China was effectively landlocked and psychologically helpless where the sea was concerned. The country was totally at the mercy of foreign naval forces, especially of the British and Japanese, and later the American, navies off the coast and up the Yangzi river.

The early warlord years coincided with the outbreak of the First World War. With all the European powers totally engaged in a life and death struggle on the battlefields of continental Europe, the military situation changed radically for China. It found the Japanese moving into the country, skillfully manipulating the rivalries among the Europeans while inserting their military forces to take the Anglo-French side, still much the stronger in the Far East, against the new power, Germany. Despite efforts by the Chinese to claim that they were on the same side during that war, the Japanese replaced the defeated forces of Germany in Shandong with their own troops when the war was over. The Chinese armies were weak and divided. The frustrations of the diplomats and the intellectuals and students who took to the streets could do little to change the situation. Nor could the Chinese trust other foreign powers to help them in their distress and humiliation. As Japan's formal allies, the British certainly did nothing to assure the Chinese of sustained support. There was no shortage of British advice, and British banks and entrepreneurs and the British government were involved in the many miscellaneous efforts to arm Chinese warlords, loan them money to buy arms and even train some of their officers and soldiers. But it was all futile and the outcome was pathetic.

Interestingly, the most likely person from the start to turn to the British for help was someone the British had learnt to distrust. This was Sun Yat-sen.[18] He was educated in English by British teachers, both in Hawaii and Hong Kong, and shared attitudes which identified him closely with the thousands of Overseas Chinese then living in various parts of the British Empire. His teacher at the Chinese Medical College in Hong Kong, Dr James Cantlie, had saved him from the Qing officials who detained him in the Chinese legation in London in 1896. Also, Sun Yat-sen was someone who had enjoyed British protection for at least part of his two and a half years' stay in British Malaya (mainly between 1908 and the end of 1910). He was given considerable freedom to travel around the colony and protectorate before his influence among his compatriots living and working under British jurisdiction made him an undesirable person there. He sought a military solution for China, to change it from an imperial monarchy to a modern republic by appealing to Western models like the French and American revolutions, and this did not endear him to the British.

Sun Yat-sen's military exploits began in 1900 and continued for another 25 years. They were largely on land, except for escapes by sea, usually in foreign vessels, when his armies failed or some of his commanders mutinied. A small number of coastal ships was made available to him by 1920. This only made him even more conscious of China's weakness at sea, and he did hope that the Military Academy he established at Huangpu would train a new generation of naval officers. There was, near the end of his life, one dramatic incident on a Chinese warship in the face of a "Leftist" plot to seize him in the early days of the Guomindang-Communist struggle for power, but he could not be said to have ever had the benefit of a navy.

For all his military actions, he received no British help, and most of his efforts were ineffectual. In any case, his own strong nationalism, and his close association with Japanese anti-Western nationalists, made him unreliable where British interests were concerned. In addition, he continued to send his ardent supporters to go among British Chinese subjects and new immigrants living in British colonies, notably to the Straits Settlements, Indian-administered Burma and Australia. This further alarmed British officials, aggravating their concerns for law and order in the plural societies under their rule. Elsewhere in Southeast Asia, Sun Yat-sen also sent his followers to Haiphong, Hanoi and Saigon in French Indo-China, but a new breed of young nationalists developed among the Chinese in the Federated Malay States, the Philippines and the Netherlands East Indies. Eventually, the British could not but notice that Singapore had become the semi-official centre in the region for the patriotic activities of Sun's political party, the Guomindang. These nationalists carefully avoided being openly anti-British, but the British and other colonial authorities found it necessary to increase their vigilance about anything to do with Sun Yat-sen.[19]

There were other reasons as well for British distrust or indifference. The political efforts by Sun Yat-sen after the 1911 revolution, accompanied by attempts to organise putative warlords and create his own fighting units, seemed burdened by incompetence. His ambitions, to put it kindly, were plagued with misfortune throughout the 1910s. At a time when British economic interests dictated the need for a stable regime in Beijing, if necessary under a friendly warlord, Sun Yat-sen was found wanting. Sun's former friends in Japan had their own agenda, not only to exploit China's weakness but also to use China's resources in order to enable Japan to be the dominant power in East Asia. Thus Sun's need for succour to create his own army, to be a "warlord" himself in an age of warlords, was ignored by both the British who had first educated him, and the Japanese who had given him his start as a revolutionary and once offered him the most encouragement.[20]

It is worth emphasising that, after the end of the First World War, the British had little to do with the Chinese ability to fight or even their desire to learn how to fight. They had been the first to introduce the Chinese to modern warfare but, having led the way into China, and already got most of what they wanted, the challenge of the other powers, notably Meiji Japan, Tsarist Russia and Bismarck's Germany, made them cautious. The tendency then was to try to support the Qing court when it was still viable and look for suitable successor regimes that they could trust to maintain order and stability so that trade could go on. The major task was to help the Chinese against further interventions and prevent the country from being carved up. In addition, Britain's own problems with its already extensive empire, and also threats from its European neighbours back home, warned the British not to get involved militarily in the Far East, but to use their skills in diplomacy instead.

When the Qing dynasty fell in 1911, Britain was no longer the most important of the powers in the Far East.

The United States had growing interests in the region and it had come to a similar conclusion that, following the 1904–1905 defeat of Tsarist Russia, their first responsibility was to save China from the Japanese. Both governments tried to limit Japan's military reach, first at the Washington Conference in 1922 and then pushing for investigations into Japan's Manchukuo adventures in 1931. After that, for a while, there was support for joining the Japanese to save China from falling into communist hands. Neither Britain nor the United States, however, was directly involved in fighting on Chinese soil during the decades leading to the second Sino-Japanese War. The most active foreign military officers in this period were Japanese, Germans, and Soviet or Comintern agents.[21] There is still a lot we do not know about those involvements. The outline of the wars they participated in has been much written about, but this is not the place to deal with those stories. The British role in the civil wars of 1912–1925 had not shaped any kind of Chinese military recovery. Their interest diminished further when the last of the warlords who had shown promise, Wu Peifu, failed to lead the forces of stability which the British supported.

And, sadly, the hopes for the one area where the British could once have given China the most valuable help, how to build a strong navy, were literally sunk with the Chinese fleet in 1895. After that, it was the one military area where the Chinese had the least opportunity to develop. For example, China's only well-known admiral, Sa Zhenbing (1859–1951), was one of the few commanders who survived the 1895 debacle. He had started his career with the birth of the Naval Academy in Mawei (Fuzhou) with Shen Baozhen and had studied

at the Royal Naval College in Greenwich. After the
Qing navy was destroyed by Japan, he worked for naval
reorganisation and his services were recognised by King
Edward VII when he led a naval mission to Britain.
Later, he rose to be Minister of the Navy under various
warlord-controlled governments in Beijing, but there
was nothing he could do to build a strong navy. None of
his students, or the junior officers who had served under
him, had the chance to earn themselves any recognition
in a service that had done nothing remarkable.[22] By the
time Admiral Sa left the navy altogether to become a
provincial governor in 1922, naval matters off the China
coast were matters entirely for the three powers, Britain,
Japan and the United States, at the Washington Conference. The Chinese had become totally irrelevant in their
own waters. It was not until decades after the communist
victory of 1949 that a truly fresh start could be made.

As for the land forces, the fundamental problem for
China before 1937 was how to get its soldiers to fight
effectively again, not only for the government forces
against their local warlord enemies but also, when the
time ultimately came to restore the country's sovereignty,
against the foreign armies on Chinese soil.[23] Neither
Sun Yat-sen and his Soviet advisers, nor Chiang Kai-
shek (1887–1975) and his German commanders, had any
idea how to restore the Chinese to the military traditions
they once had, notably the fearsome and dedicated fighting skills of the Manchu Bannermen before 1800. What
they had to offer in institutions like the Huangpu Military Academy, and all the smaller academies and training
schools that were established in various provinces, were
new methods of conducting war and how to fight with
the latest weaponry. These institutions served largely to

train officers how to defeat the immediate enemy, the
warlords during the Northern Expedition and the communist armies of the Jiangxi Soviets. There was never
time nor resources enough to build up a new tradition
of career service, of the necessary professional pride that
would overcome the historical reluctance to allow bright
young men to become soldiers.

But two developments laid the foundation for a new
burst of fighting energy among the Chinese people. First
was the mobilisation of the peasantry for both a patriotic
war against the Japanese and, in the best traditional style,
a rebellion against landlords and corrupt officials plus –
using the new rhetoric of revolution – their treacherous
bourgeois pro-imperialist allies. This was not a great military tradition but, following the Long March that the
communist armies made to the northwest in 1935, the
experience revived and modernised older ideas about
how the militarily weak could fight orthodox armies
with guerrilla tactics and, if necessary, with overwhelming numbers.[24] Secondly, a new Pacific power was born
from the attack on Pearl Harbor in 1941 and this led to
full-scale United States support for the modernisation
of the Chinese armies of the Nationalist government in
Chungking.

But the picture was not simple. At one level, the
British Empire began to reemerge as the Commonwealth. At another level, highlighted by the Atlantic
Alliance against Germany on the European continent,
an informal empire was taking shape to assume some of
the responsibilities that the British Empire had created
world-wide over the past century. An American "empire de facto" started out on the Far East periphery and
eventually succeeded that of a very real British Empire,

one that took over the China connection and extended it further than the British ever tried to do. In the larger global framework, such a view would offer a credible angle of vision. It is no accident that Winston Churchill (1874–1965) came out of the war writing the history of the English-speaking peoples. And, as the empire began to shrink and Britain's destiny came to be more closely linked to the European continent, there was no shortage of British opinion that encouraged a more benign attitude towards the colony (or thirteen colonies) that got away. The rise of American studies in British universities in the 1950s marked a pronounced shift in perspective. The acknowledgment that American literary and political figures were worthy of close study and the wider acceptance of American scholarship about British and European history and current affairs confirmed what Churchill had highlighted. The United States offered new standards of wealth and power which more and more British people admired, whether they liked it or not.

In turn, President Franklin D. Roosevelt (1882–1945) and his successors overcame America's historic aversion to involvement in Old World affairs and took the final step towards the "manifest destiny" thrust upon them in East Asia at the turn of the twentieth century. There was no turning back. And what better way to take on the "white man's burden" than to learn from the British and try on their shoes? No doubt there was no exact fit. No doubt the American way had a different mix of fighting, trading, converting and ruling. But much of the British experience, the institutional structures that were still viable, could be used as a basis for creating more informal but equally resilient connections.

Where China and the Chinese were concerned, there were significant differences in both history and geography to be taken into account. And this impacted immediately upon the military commitment that the Americans could, and were willing to, put into the Chinese cause.

Thus "to fight" in Anglo-Chinese relations took on new dimensions following the outbreak of the second Sino-Japanese War in 1937. Before Pearl Harbor, support for China was still minimal, low-key and largely covert. Both the British and the Americans were sensitive to the dual threats of a fascist and militarist Japan allied to Germany on the one hand and Soviet international communism on the other. They saw that they could most help China by propping up the Nationalist forces that would resist both those enemies of Anglo-American interests and political culture. For Roosevelt more than for Churchill, the goal was a strong and united China that could stand up to those hostile forces and become a long-term ally. It was a goal worth fighting for. It was worth investing money and resources to equip and train the Nationalist armies and air force.[25] The immediate result was to tie down Japanese troops in China and make it easier to drive back their forces elsewhere in Asia and the Pacific. For the future, it was hoped that the newly strengthened armies would be able to defeat the communists and unite the country under a friendly Chiang Kai-shek national government.

Ever since the defeat by Japan in 1895, there had not been a serious role for the Chinese navy. Chinese waters were totally out of Chinese control while the warlords fought one another for supremacy on land. The British continued to sell or help build a few small ships and offer training to under-funded naval and coastal units. But the warlords, and the Nationalists after 1928, were plagued by civil wars and never had the resources to revive the country's naval arm. With the Japanese invasion, the isolation from the sea was complete. No part of the China coast could be said to be under Chinese jurisdiction. If there was any fighting to be done, China was left, more than ever before, to defend itself in a continental war. Never before had the Chinese military been less connected to maritime concerns. It was not merely weakness at sea and disastrous defeats that were exceptional. It was the unprecedented dependence on foreign allies to save China, with their navies winning at sea against China's enemies. For China itself, the only strategy was to trade land for ultimate survival, rather like Tsarist Russia facing the armies of Napoleon. But, unlike Russia, China has always had a long coastline, many excellent and ice-free ports and at times a formidable navy. Its failure to take advantage of British skills when it could have done had left it prostrate like a wounded beached whale. Was it to be the United States that would try to get it afloat again?

When the Second World War ended with Allied victory, the Chinese Nationalist government failed to stop the communist armies. Some of its sailors had been trained by the British before and during the war. These were put to use, together with massive American support, to move whole Nationalist armies to thwart the communist guerrilla forces that were heading towards territories which had been held by the Japanese. In 1945–1949, a small navy, which the Americans and the British had helped to refit, was put together with Japanese ships left with the Chinese after the war. The

flotillas of Japanese ships and those provided with British
and American help totalled some 400 ships, with over
250 of them supposedly in battle-ready condition. That
makeshift fleet totalled some 190,000 tons and carried
over 40,000 men. But it was largely the American vessels and planes which transported Nationalist troops to
Manchuria and other battlefronts. Chinese sources at
the time claimed that some 540,000 troops were thus
transported. This navy was thought to have been strong
enough to blockade the coasts from Fujian to Liaodong
peninsula. For example, six out of the nine vessels of
the Second Fleet that had gone over to the communists in 1949 were sunk by the navy that stayed loyal
to the Nationalist government. The remnants of the
force were strong enough to fight off the attempts by the
People's Liberation Army (PLA) to take Denglu Island
off the coast of Zhejiang. They also won a major battle
at Jinmen (Quemoy) island off Xiamen, with heavy PLA
losses of over 9,000 men.[26] But these victories could not
save the Nationalists.

When the war went badly for the Guomindang government in Nanjing, the navy was also used to help ship
the retreating armies, senior members of the government
and some of the country's national treasures to Taiwan.
But the end of foreign presence in China's inland waters
was near. The last British naval encounter with Communist Chinese troops was the so-called "Amethyst" incident on the Yangzi. The British may stress the dignified
retreat and the courage of the sailors involved and the
Chinese their indignation at residual British presump-
tions, but it truly brought to a close the "fighting" phase
of encounters begun with the "Opium War" 109 years
earlier.[27] No naval forces were employed by the PLA

because it had no navy. But the incident provided its Eastern China Command with the impetus to establish its first naval force. The new headquarters of the virtual navy was located at Baima temple in Taizhou, Jiangsu, just north of where the *Amethyst* was first attacked. This Command was to get a substantial start soon afterwards when it received the surrender of Nationalist gunboats of the Second Fleet and the Fifth Patrol fleet.

By December 1949, Xiao Jingguang had been made Admiral and Head of the Navy and it was soon decided that the PLA would have to learn from the Soviet navy. Xiao Jingguang was a Huangpu Academy graduate, with no naval background but with eight years' experience in the Soviet Union. His main deputy, however, was trained in the Voroshilov Naval Academy from 1953 to 1957, and so were most of the active commanders who succeeded them. The Russians were invited to send hundreds of officers and experts to serve in China and, between 1951 and 1953, the PLA also sent about 150 officers to Russia for training.

This was another new beginning for China's navy.[28] The communists' armies were modern peasant rebels hardened by guerrilla tactics, inspired by fervent political ideals, and their fighting ability enhanced by modern weaponry and training. Their victory in 1949, except for the crossing over to Hainan Island, was won entirely on land. They did inherit some of the naval craft from the defeated Nationalists, but they were totally cut off from Anglo-American and Japanese naval traditions and skills. Their most powerful ally, Soviet Russia, was not renowned for its naval prowess. But these Russians would have to do. Their eastern fleet in Vladivostok could provide help, and other ships were for the key

early years actually in Chinese ports like Port Arthur
on the Liaodong peninsula. But that is another story. In
the face of the new Anglo-Chinese relationship forming across the Taiwan Straits, one in which naval forces
would play an increasingly important part, the People's
Republic of China (PRC) would come to experience
both frustration and challenge.

After its withdrawal from the Yangzi, Britain adopted
a neutralist role in Hong Kong. Waiting to observe if the
Chinese navy would stay loyal to the Guomindang government, to see how many fighting ships would actually
follow the regime offshore, was one of the dramas of the
day. It was understandable that Britain would wish to restrain naval actions off the southern Chinese coast in the
face of the petty rivalries within the Chinese navy and
the Nanking government's distrust at the time of many of
its naval officers. Too many of them had gone over to the
communists and it took years for a new trusted generation to be trained. Nevertheless, what China's small naval
units, now on both sides of the Taiwan Straits, were able
to do marked a turnaround in modern Chinese history.
Not since the exploits of Zheng Chenggong (Koxinga),
the Fujian trader-sailor who created China's first offshore
navy in the seventeenth century and based it in Taiwan,
had Chinese naval power been so effective. The retreat to
Taiwan opened a new opportunity for seaborne fighting for the Chinese. At long last, the Anglo-Chinese
connection could focus on the greatest strength of the
British heritage, which the Americans also share, and
lead the Chinese to rethink security and strategy in a
fundamentally different way.

But here is the greatest irony. After the British had
stopped fighting the Chinese for decades, after their

American successors had helped to strengthen Chinese armies to fight the Japanese as well as other Chinese, the opportunity and need had finally come for Chinese on the mainland to take naval power seriously. The very untidiness that left the Nationalists on islands like Matsu and Quemoy symbolises that new start. The PRC's failure to take both these islands underlined the urgency to produce new plans to take Taiwan. This had to include a modern navy. After the Korean War, with the stationing of the Seventh Fleet in the Taiwan Straits, the Americans had become a direct threat to the new regime of Mao Zedong. The heightening of Cold War tensions around the globe led the United States to make the China seas and their outreach southwards the new front line that encompassed Southeast Asia and Australia.

The People's Liberation Army did indeed learn much from Soviet Russia where air force designs, missile weaponry and the products of nuclear engineering were concerned. The Sino-Soviet connection was, for at least one decade, greatly valued. But as two major continental powers with different national interests in Eurasia and the world's longest land borders, the friendship was too good to last. Within a decade, the two sides found the innate contradictions too difficult to live with. As a superpower, the Soviet Union had other regions to satisfy and China's particular concerns did not always serve the Russian cause. As long as Russia was the stronger of the two, but not overwhelmingly dominant, the break between the two communist powers was inevitable.[29] In any case, China's ability to fight was greatly weakened by the Soviet withdrawal of technology and vital skilled personnel in 1960. It was not until after Deng Xiaoping's reforms following the Cultural Revolution that the PRC could start again to think about how the country could be defended in the future.

This is not the place to dwell on China's military history. I only wish to highlight, where fighting was concerned, the complex Chinese responses to the Anglo-Chinese experience. Britain was the first modern enemy, but the Qing court was willing to learn from the British how to strengthen its armed forces, including the navy. But that failed, and China was forced to endure desperate measures barely to survive for at least the next sixty years. Having failed to find a new attitude towards naval strength from the years when Britain was at the height of its powers, the Chinese then saw the growing irrelevance of Britain to their fighting ability. One might conclude that this fact would end our story, but two reasons lead me to suggest that there has been a new beginning. The image of China's navy, its feeble rise and precipitous fall, its virtual disappearance, and then its rebirth since 1949 in both Taiwan and in the PRC, captures the layers of fighting encounters which we should not neglect. It tells us something about the ambiguities that China has been, and is still going through, but it also tells us something about the ambivalence in Britain's position between the continent and the beckoning Atlantic.

Perhaps the most important question is whether, as a result of this two-stage Anglo-Chinese relationship, leaping from an Atlantic Britain to a Pacific United States, the Chinese government will fundamentally shift away from its continental traditions to embrace naval power and the multiple challenges posed by the sea. The issue of reunifying the province of Taiwan with the mainland is a vexatious one. Increasingly, China may have to look beyond simply strengthening its navy and preparing to use ballistic missiles to overcome its intrinsic naval weaknesses. But, even if that should happen, it is unlikely that the recent efforts to develop a blue water navy will slow down. In the long run, with the country's long coastline, China cannot do without a credible naval defence capability. As this capability grows, more Chinese naval vessels can be expected to use the sea-lanes of the South China Sea. This will have an impact on how the control of the Spratly Islands might eventually be shared. There is no real alternative to this development because the Chinese cannot now unlearn the lesson the British had taught them that they should never again leave the soft coastal underbelly vulnerable to external invasion.[30]

There is ample evidence that, when they have the need to, Chinese people can turn to the sea. It is a matter of whether they can make a national commitment. There have been significant numbers of navy officers who were recruited from north, central and western China to dispel the view that sailors have to come from the coastal regions. Nevertheless, there is ample evidence of keen response to naval careers among the young people in Taiwan as well as among the Chinese Singaporeans who command and man that republic's small but efficient navy. Many of them have ancestors who came from southern Fujian, the area from which intrepid sailors had ventured north and southwards for centuries.

It is not too fanciful to compare the Hokkiens, in their southeastern corner of the continent, with the Dutch and the Portuguese during the sixteenth and seventeenth centuries. Their destinies were to look seaward and they could have evolved systematically in that direction had they not been so grounded by an orthodox agrarian worldview that was firmly rooted on land. The resource the Hokkiens offered was relatively untapped by the imperial authorities in the past, although their contribution to coastal defence had always been appreciated. Official neglect of their talents, however, had not prevented these Hokkiens from honing their skills for overseas trading purposes.[31] Here they have had more in common with the commercial traditions of the British. Perhaps in this realm, Anglo-Chinese relations might have been more fruitful. This leads to the second of Waley's four words, "to trade".

3 "To trade"

Towards the end of chapter two, I painted a picture of British naval power in retreat and the rise of American power in the Pacific on the eve of the Second World War. This did not represent a sunset phase for the Commonwealth's links with China. It may have seemed like that where military involvement was concerned, but it was certainly not so with trade. On the contrary, there was a new beginning for other parts of the Commonwealth like Australia and residual colonies like Hong Kong and Malaya (including Singapore), plus the new economic power of English-speaking North America. British traders and officials had left structures around the Asia-Pacific region that were ready to take over and continue their globalising missions. The question was how China would respond.

Let me begin by juxtaposing two historical notes. First, the continental Chinese could not be more different from the island British. It is not surprising that they should develop their trading methods differently. But there were Chinese who were more like other Europeans from the point of view of geography, of the response to political conditions, and of human resources. For example, in my earlier writings, I drew a comparison between the Hokkiens in southeastern Fujian (and one might include the Cantonese of the Pearl River delta) and the Dutch and Portuguese during the sixteenth and seventeenth centuries. Their respective destinies for some centuries had been to look seaward from the edge of a continent. The Dutch and Portuguese rulers freed themselves from control by their land-based neighbours to send out overseas merchants with naval backing. The enterprising traders of Fujian and Guangdong, however, set out to take great risks overseas while being constrained by rulers and mandarins who held an orthodox agrarian worldview that was firmly rooted to the soil.[1]

The Hokkiens and Cantonese did nevertheless develop maritime and trading skills and offered their talents to their imperial authorities whenever these were needed. But the skills were relatively untapped by the dynastic authorities. Such official neglect did not prevent them from drawing on their experiences in the region to deal with the Portuguese and the Dutch. These foreign protagonists off the China coast were, like themselves, edge-of-continent peoples who had overcome their handicaps on land by becoming masters of the oceans. Centuries earlier, in the tenth century, beginning with their respective independent southern Han (917–971) and Min (909–944) empires, both the Cantonese and Hokkien had shown their strength in long-distance seaborne trade. They were able to match the Indians, Persians and Arabs by trading beyond the South China Sea into the Indian Ocean and were eventually stopped from doing so only by the continental policy introduced when the Ming dynasty (1368–1644) reunified the empire.[2] This new policy was based on the idea that China's markets were so attractive to foreign rulers and merchants that it was safer for the empire, and more profitable for the officials concerned, to restrain their own coastal traders and let the foreigners come to China and shoulder all the risks. This way, the mandarins could also better control all the troublesome people, Chinese and non-Chinese alike, who were motivated merely by trading profits.

My second historical note brings us to the present and relates to the description of China as the last market frontier during the debates on admitting China into the World Trade Organisation. This was when the US Congress finally overcame strong moral and political resistance to vote for permanent normal trading relations with the People's Republic of China. That description reminds me of the perennial image of China as a country of "400 million customers". The famous book of that title may have appeared only in 1937, but the image of a vast virgin market for the industrialised West had been around for at least a hundred years before that.[3] Now that the population of China has tripled (to 1.3 billion), this powerful call to cross the last frontier sounds more attractive than ever. When one traces decisions made to open up the China market back to all those centuries when foreign traders knocked on the door of China, it is no wonder that Chinese coastal peoples expected maritime trade to profit them and Chinese governments believed that trade was too important to leave to merchants. It is a reminder that it took more than 320 years, from the Portuguese arrival to the Opium War, before the West could push themselves into the China market, a little more than 100 years after that for the market to close down again in 1949, and then another 22 years for the doors to reopen after 1978. Behind all the debates over the centuries, we should remember that China's trade has never been far from issues of power and security and that it does not take much for that trade to be shut down again. This is also the reason why the market reopened guardedly after 1978 and through the 1990s, and why it still sometimes resembles the controlled trading system that the British found so irksome in the nineteenth century. With China's entry into the WTO, of course, a new chapter begins. But it may be a long while before China will allow its economy to be as open as some businesses want.

It is with that background in mind that we turn to the words, "to trade". The desire "to trade" has always been more central to British interests than the readiness "to fight". Here is a paradox. On the one hand, the British carried the burden of having started the modern round of wars in China. On the other, the record shows how hard the British tried to stop any fighting that would inhibit their trade in China. The contrast has not been lost among the Chinese. The dichotomous image meets both the need for a symbol to unite an easily divided population and for a spur to Chinese businessmen to beat the British peacefully with China's own long-established business skills and networks. Certainly, Chinese traders saw how much they could have had in common with the commercial traditions of the British. Unlike that of fighting, this is a realm where Anglo-Chinese relations could have been much more fruitful. Chinese official classes were struck by the wealth that overseas commercial enterprises could produce, and this prepared them to review the lowly status of their merchants and seek to redefine the roles that these merchants could play in China's national development.

Today, Chinese businessmen are listed among the world's billionaire entrepreneurs. Many of the most successful are socially respected and popularly admired. They have greatly improved their access to power and are even regularly consulted by political leaders both within and outside their countries. It is hard to believe that, not that long ago, merchants in China were despised by those in power. For hundreds of years, they were carefully controlled and denied entrance into the political establishment. A remarkable change occurred during the twentieth century. The entrepreneurial class has now established a role in politics unthinkable at the beginning of the millennium. Many have become essential to systems of power where they had once been subject to the whims of rulers, courtiers and the literate elites. After centuries spent struggling vainly for status, the merchants began in the twentieth century to transform their relations with those in power. Many still start from humble beginnings, but more are now better educated and have received various kinds of formal training. They are increasingly expected to play public roles, some of which would prepare them to be partners in the power structures of the new millennium.

Why, then, did I start with fighting and not with trade? After all, the British and the Chinese traded for at least two centuries before they went to war. Did the British, with their East India Company, not have something to teach the Chinese decades before the end of the eighteenth century? Were they not better traders from at least that time? If the Chinese had learnt to trade like them earlier, perhaps they would not have had to fight. The simple answer is that this was not how the Chinese saw it before the second half of the nineteenth century.

It was not until late in that century that they began
to acknowledge that there was something about British
methods of trading that was worth learning. And even
till this day many have argued that the learning that had
to be done was not all one way. The Chinese experience
itself has much to offer the modern trading world.[4]

No one doubts today that where fighting is concerned, China has had to learn from the Anglo traditions and will have much more to learn, especially from
English-speaking Americans, for a long while to come.
But where trading was concerned, Chinese merchants
did not think that they were in any way backward, especially those hardy ones of the southern coasts who traded
overseas in Southeast Asia without official approval.
I mentioned that Chinese mandarins were impressed
that British merchants could produce so much wealth
through overseas enterprises. Insofar as these mandarins
saw that trade as the work of a dominant monopolistic
company like the East India Company, this conformed
to their view that all foreign trade was best conducted by
the rulers in a similar monopoly through their control-
lable merchants. For the Chinese merchants, the fact that
the English company had naval support was proof that
official endorsements made all the difference. What was
new for the Chinese court was the idea that these foreign rulers would fight for their merchants so that they
could trade successfully. This was something inconceiv-
able to them.[5] And Chinese historians to this day remain
sceptical of the idea that the British used force for the
opening of China merely for a free trade ideal in support of merchants and not because they wanted more
profits for their ruling classes by selling opium to the
Chinese.

The British have always insisted that the issue was the protection of the new progressive ideas of open trading rights. The history of the English East India Company is a story of how the British sought to compete with its European rivals, notably the impetus following the defeat of the Spanish armada and the success of the Dutch against the Portuguese in India and the East Indies. Trade supported by the state arose in response to political conditions in Western Europe. The rise of the London merchant in English politics led to the use of armed trading vessels backed by the state. Although this may have seemed, at the beginning, little more than sanctioned piracy that enriched rulers and merchants alike, the armed merchant ships were ultimately regulated in order that they performed only defensive tasks. Thus, in British eyes, their ships bringing goods to Chinese shores were not evidence of a sudden exercise of naval power but of a search for normal trading rights.[6] If this forced the Chinese rulers to do the necessary economic engineering to preserve the livelihood of their merchants, that was part of progress.

If we look at the way the Chinese entrepreneurs use their extensive networks today, we would not say that the British model of the global trading company has anything to do with Chinese business ways. Indeed, the roots of trading among the Chinese go back a long way. At the heart of their learning experiences was the fact that they were a despised class in the eyes of imperial mandarins and had to make their way without any help from the authorities. If anything, the tradition was that their activities were permitted by the court only because some trade was necessary, but the court reserved the right to restrain them whenever it decided that what the merchants did was not helpful to the realm. In the meantime, they could be exploited by the ruling elites for defence, philanthropic and revenue purposes. This was especially true of foreign trade, which the emperors sought to control throughout the centuries.[7] When trading with foreigners, the rulers assumed that they were dealing with the agents of foreign rulers. Therefore, they thought it natural that the court should determine the limits of that trade in the interests of national security. This had always been so along the land borders of the empire where tribal kingdoms wanted more trade than China was prepared to allow, and Chinese emperors decided to fight them and drive them away. This was no less true of the coastal regions.

In other words, the Chinese court always understood that foreign rulers wanted trade and, therefore, chose to treat all merchant ships as trading on behalf of their rulers. The matter, therefore, was one between rulers and could be dealt with as one concerning ruler-to-ruler relations. Each ruler was then placed in a hierarchy of relationships in a tributary system the Chinese devised in which the emperor placed himself at the top, above the rest. The foreign rulers were allotted positions relative to their location and distance from China, to their size and wealth and to their importance to China's diplomatic and defence needs.[8]

Thus, to the Chinese rulers, the English East India Company was no different from earlier traders, and its agents were treated as representatives of the king of England. The idea that they could trade directly with private Chinese merchants was unacceptable. And, had they been seen as mere representatives of a group of merchants in London, their status would have been

even lower. Therefore, a group of Chinese merchants in
Canton, licensed as the gonghang or Cohong (which
meant that the group operated a court-devised trading
system), was assigned to deal with them under close
official supervision.[9] When Lord Macartney was sent
as a representative of the king of England, the Chinese
assumed that he wanted the status of the trade raised so
that England's rights under the tributary system could
be improved. Recent research has shown that the Qing
emperors were not anti-merchants and did have practical
ideas about raising revenues through domestic trade and
thus developing the national economy. But this was not
extended to trade with foreigners. What the Qianlong
emperor could not accept was that the system of foreign
trade should be changed to enable private merchants on
both sides to trade freely, with only customs officials in
charge. He had difficulty understanding that these foreign rulers would protect the interests of traders as a
matter of policy, even of principle. And the hardest part
for the Chinese to believe was that a country would go
to war for trade, for the sake of merchants.[10]

It would be wrong to say that the Chinese did not
have a strong trading tradition at sea. But this trade was
carried on under extremely difficult conditions. For the
Chinese and the British to trade freely, there had to
be more independent maritime activity on the part of
the Chinese. To appreciate the extent to which the
Chinese changed their attitudes towards foreign trade,
and to see the British contribution to that change, we
need to present a fuller picture here.

I have noted how maritime China was constrained
by the tributary system of a continental empire. The
system was based on the idea of concentric circles,

with the centre made up of the lands of the Son of
Heaven. Next in order of proximity were Chinese feudal lords and princes, followed by minor chieftains on
the Chinese borders. These were followed by more dis-
tant rulers of kingdoms who wanted a relationship with
China and who were prepared to send tribute to the
emperor. When the Chinese reached the whole length
of the coasts from the Liaodong peninsula to the Gulf of
Tongking, they expanded the system to include rulers
who were prepared to send ships to open relations and
trade with China.[11] Thus they used the one formula to
serve both land and sea relationships.

In practice, there were differences, the most important of which was that it became accepted wisdom that
those who came by sea could occasionally create trouble
but were no real threats to the empire. The sea borders were easier to defend than the overland routes into
China, the foreign ships were small, the trading fleets
carried more goods and merchants than armed soldiers
or sailors, and these were not capable of endangering
the throne. In this system, maritime China was that segment of the imperial realm dedicated to naval defence,
diplomatic relations and merchant control. The people
concerned were mainly mandarins, military officials and
select merchants as well as their foreign counterparts.
This maritime trade grew during the first millennium
and became important during the Song and Yuan dynasties. By that time, the Chinese had a large and powerful navy and this enabled the Mongol Yuan to organise
world-conquering forays across Asian waters to Japan
(1274 and 1281), to the Indo-China coasts (1283–1287)
and then to Java (1292–1293).[12] Although ultimately un-
successful, they encouraged many more Chinese to be

drawn into larger maritime enterprises. This was often done together with those Muslim traders who had been drawn to China by land and by sea because of the Pax Mongolica that the Yuan emperors extended to all of China. The climax of this development saw the fitting out of the seven voyages of Admiral Zheng He during the early half of the fifteenth century (1405–1433). The expeditions made regular visits to key rulers in Southeast Asia and the southern coastal kingdoms of South Asia. At least four of them reached the Red Sea port cities of West Asia and the coast of East Africa. At their strongest, the expeditions involved over 27,000 men in 62 large ships accompanied by hundreds of smaller vessels. The impact of this spectacular display of naval power was largely symbolic and political and was not directed to enhancing Chinese trade in the region.[13]

What might have been a natural progression to more maritime commitments did not happen. The voyages were stopped in 1433. The founder of the Ming dynasty had, in 1368, after recovering Han Chinese control from the Mongols, restructured the tributary system to control all foreign trade more tightly than ever before. Maritime China thus became a segment of a carefully regulated security system. In this context, the Zheng He expeditions might not appear to accord with the new policy, but they were official missions and there were no concessions made to private overseas trade. By the end of the Xuande reign (1424–1435), the policy laid down by the founder of the Ming dynasty was clearly reaffirmed. During the next century, the coming of the Portuguese and the Spanish and the activities of the Wako (gangs of Japanese and Chinese pirates) along the whole China coast did draw fresh imperial attention to coastal defence. There was some relaxation of merchant control after 1567 and this stimulated a burst of trading activities.[14] What was significant, however, was that Ming China maintained its tribute-centred maritime policy and that the successor Qing rulers adopted the essentials of a similar policy.

Qing officials were more flexible towards foreign traders, but there was no shift away from the forms of the tributary system. Even after it became clear by the end of the eighteenth century that the English East India Company had become the dominant trading power in the region, the Qing mandarins recommended no change to the trading structure. This position continued until past the Treaty of Nanking of 1842. Even then, many officials continued to adopt a negative policy towards foreign trade, but some had begun to recommend that the Qing court adopt a more proactive policy. But the rhetoric employed made it clear that maritime China remained a small segment of a larger system of defence, diplomacy and trade.

The people of the coastal provinces had been pushing out seaward despite this inward-looking centripetal policy and were eager to trade with foreign merchants coming by sea. They had built networks linking them to various Muslim groups from the Indian Ocean, to Japanese, Indians and some Southeast Asians. When the Dutch and the English arrived, it coincided with a weakening of central authority. The court in Beijing was distracted by vicious political infighting and widespread internal rebellions. These were followed by the Manchu invasion. It was not an easy time for officials to retain control of an increasingly disorderly and boisterous coastal China. Hence the rise of Zheng Zhilong (d. 1661) and

his son, Zheng Chenggong (Koxinga), and their many
rivals, and the intensification of Iberian-Dutch competition at Macau and then in Taiwan. Although Ming
officials were alerted to such dangers to their traditional
policy, there was little they could do to curb the increasingly violent activities along the whole length of their
coastal domains.

Undoubtedly, when the centre was weak, the periphery thrived. For more than half a century, from the 1620s
to 1684, maritime China could be described as a region in flames. The Zheng family built up their armed
trading fleet, one of the most powerful in the world
at the time and more than a match against the navies
of the Spanish and the Dutch far from their bases at
home. The Zheng naval forces were raiding freely along
the coasts and stimulating Chinese-led trade on a scale
never seen before. This was a chance for maritime China
to become a major player in Asian history. From foreign
records, like those of the Japanese, the Dutch and the
Spanish, it looked like the beginnings of a new era for
the maritime peoples of China.[15] But this was not to
be. The major difference was that the Chinese armed
merchants were themselves a serious danger to Chinese
imperial authority, and the rulers, whether Han Chinese
or Manchu, were determined to destroy them. In addition to fighting their European rivals, the Zheng forces
had to defend themselves against the triumphant Qing
forces after 1644. The Qing court eventually defeated
the Zheng regime in Taiwan and brought the region
firmly under central control. There was thus a complete
restoration of a continental normalcy. But neither mainland Fujian Chinese, nor those who survived in Taiwan
and those who went there in the following centuries,

were to forget that they once had a naval tradition that served them well both in war and commerce.

What of the century from 1750 to 1850, the first half of which saw the Qing empire at the peak of its power while the second saw it weaken rapidly? Conventionally, the rebellions of the 1800s could be interpreted as manifestations of downturn in the dynastic cycle. But this was also a time when foreign trade continued to grow. For example, the bulk seaborne trade in rice was flourishing, the fluctuations in the price of overseas silver were normal, there was steady growth in transactions using the official Canton trading system at the expense of Macau, and the peopling by Chinese of Taiwan and Southeast Asian ports continued apace.[16]

The English East India Company (EIC) and the country traders whom it spawned had become dominant groups on the China coast. The country traders, in particular, had learnt to deal with the growing number of their Chinese counterparts, what Hao Yen-p'ing calls the "shopmen", the "outside merchants" who operated successfully outside the Cohong system.[17] Like their countrymen from the provinces of Fujian and Guangdong who ranged widely across the ocean to Japan, the Philippines, Thailand and the Malay Archipelago, these coastal traders had shaken off some of the traditional official constraints to seek out interlocking relationships with the foreign traders who needed their services. Unlike in Southeast Asia, however, there were no higher European authorities on the China coast that could interfere with their commerce. The Chinese merchants, therefore, had superior bargaining power for several decades prior to the outbreak of the Opium War. In the course of these years of cooperation, various kinds of Anglo-Chinese partnerships were formed, and the partners found much to learn from each other's trading ways. Acting together, each partnership competed with the EIC and Cohong merchants and others like themselves to expand their ventures along the coast. Wherever possible, the country traders could also count on their "shopmen" links to reach some of the markets in the interior of China. After the end of the East India Company's monopoly in 1833, an even greater variety of such creative partnerships was established. These profitable experiences laid foundations for the "commercial revolution" that was to create a new kind of Chinese merchant class on the China coast. These were men who understood their Western counterparts, notably the British and the Americans, and who were not afraid of the fierce competitions that now became the norm. Beyond the reach of the mandarins in Beijing and the provincial capitals, they were ready to take full advantage of the new opportunities created by the war of 1840–1842, and the even more extensive ones offered by the enforced peace of the 1860s.[18]

The mandarin-dominated system that controlled commerce ineffectively at the various ports took little note of the beginnings of the radical change taking place among the private traders. That system continued to shackle the Cohong merchants. Malpractices between them and the mandarins in charge ensured that profits were uncertain and that new initiatives were discouraged. Neither the Canton authorities nor the EIC merchants were satisfied with the conditions. When the EIC lost its monopoly and ever more foreign traders sought Chinese partners outside the system, the government became obsessed with trade deficits and the moral ramifications of the opium trade. There was little new thinking about what to do; the emperor and his officials thought only of reasserting full control. Clearly, the breakdown of authority had bred ever more greed. As a result, southern China became poorer and more disorderly, the Canton merchants were continually in debt, and the imperial and provincial customs offices were more threatened by corruption than ever. For many, change was necessary and inevitable.[19]

Among the Chinese actually living abroad, the communities in Java and the nearby islands were recovering from the Batavia massacre of 1743. They had adapted themselves to local conditions with courage and imagination, notably in West Borneo, in the Riau-Johore empire, in Semarang and Central Java, and even in Melaka on the Malay Peninsula. In Manila, the Chinese who survived a brief period of British occupation were at the mercy of the Spanish once more.[20] Nevertheless, the Chinese records of this period show that these communities were keenly aware of their positions outside the emperor's reach, they were weaned from old habits of self-restraint, and this enabled them to extend the networking that became a major source of their trading strength.

Two other developments point to even more important changes. Firstly, the role that the Chinese played in the new Siamese power restored at Thonburi-Bangkok and, secondly, the free trade doctrines that accompanied British advances on the Malay Peninsula, at Penang and later at Singapore. They provided the framework for the two dominant patterns of Chinese settlement in Southeast Asia. The first advanced the Chinese role in a new Thai polity, the transition of maritime Chinese to become Southeast Asian urban and rural settlers, and their evolution into strong merchant groups who maintained special relations with China. The second pattern, of free trade in Penang and Singapore, saw the establishment of new kinds of bases for maritime Chinese commerce. These two ports provided the first chance the Chinese had ever had to become majority groups in territories outside the Chinese empire's jurisdiction.[21]

In 1800, no one could have foreseen the era of wars that was to bring imperial China down later in the nineteenth century. But, among those Chinese who were living outside the empire, they were aware that a new age was dawning. Also, increasing numbers of southern coast Chinese understood that, when they could not realise their ambitions on Chinese soil itself, they could bring their dreams with them overseas. Here the British contribution was clear. Trading with the Chinese after the 1840s in ports from Shanghai and Tianjin down to Singapore and Penang, whether under their jurisdiction or not, gave the British considerable leverage in the developments to come.

It may seem, from the above account, that the key initiatives for action had come from the foreigners trading in China. But we should note how the Chinese middlemen and their junks achieved a central position amongst the foreign traders. They had found new strategies that enabled them to deal with the rapid changes. They became confident of their importance to the Europeans when they found the measure of the Dutch and British merchant administrators. Locally based Chinese merchants had mastered some Western practices and their laws. They had worked out the subtleties between partnership and collaboration, and made their newly acquired knowledge the foundations of the trading ties they needed for dealing with their home ports in China.[22] The half-century before the British opening of the Treaty Ports in 1842 may be described as the golden age of "sojourner networking". During this period, the Chinese gained an autonomous place under Dutch and British commercial and naval hegemony. In maritime Southeast Asia, far from their emperor's control, these floating maritime Chinese had several decades to prepare themselves for the changes to come. They were ready for the spectacular decade of the 1850s, when the massive exodus of Chinese occurred, not only across the South China Sea, but also across the Pacific Ocean.

By the time the Treaty Ports were opened to international trade, no one doubted that the British were better fighters. But few Chinese would agree that they were better traders. They would continue to think that the British navy gave their merchants unfair advantages. This was a lesson that the Japanese were quick to learn as their ruling elites wasted little time and trained naval forces to support their capitalist ventures. The Qing government, however, in its last days, and the Republic during its first decades, talked much about adopting the models of modern enterprises. The models they had in mind were exemplified by British companies set up in Shanghai, cross-linked with those in Hong Kong, Singapore or the ports of India and, ultimately, to the city of London. Men like Li Hongzhang (1823–1901), Sheng Xuanhuai (1844–1916) and Zhang Jian (1853–1926) began to build government-backed companies. The China Merchants' Steam Navigation Company and the Kiangnan Arsenal provided early models. Many others were started in the coal and iron, cotton and textiles, shipping and transport industries. These evolved into a variety of mandarin-merchant cooperative ventures, but these new organisations never overcame some basic limitations.[23] They represented an official Chinese response to the idea of large joint-stock companies, but the experiments were always top down and never went much beyond the direct supervision of merchants.

What also became clear to Chinese entrepreneurs was that, when China became obviously weaker, they became less able to do business with Western agency houses on equal terms. By the early 1880s, trading conditions for the Chinese worsened. After China's defeat by the French in 1884, and even more so after the defeat by the Japanese in 1894–1895, merchants with industrial and financial ambitions found that Western firms enjoyed unfair advantages guaranteed by the Treaty Ports and by their official connections with a powerful international system. This led the Chinese to be increasingly aware that a supportive state was necessary to enable them to compete at all. Once the mandarins themselves realised this as well, the seeds of economic nationalism were sown. This went hand-in-hand with the nationalist awakening that accompanied the debates about trade as an extension of war, about competitive trading as another kind of fighting, and how this new kind of mercantile war (*shangzhan*) should be fought.

For the Chinese private traders themselves, this remained largely talk and debate. The kind of support they might have hoped for never materialised. There was little legal protection for joint-stock companies, and financing methods through modern banks were slow to develop. The difficulty in ensuring that local capital be channelled to Chinese businesses became greater.

In addition, the lack of trust beyond strong kinship systems meant that the new bourgeoisie could not move away from their traditional family businesses even if they were convinced that they should to be truly competitive against foreign competition. In order to survive, they increased the range of their business networks and, as methods of transport and communication improved, they further refined and strengthened these through enlarging their circles of clan or native-place connections.

In short, the Chinese did have something to learn from the great British companies. The lessons came in three stages. First, the country needed to see trade as essential to national interest and, therefore, worth defending and fighting for. This was understood by the second decade of the twentieth century when official encouragement was given to the large number of modern businesses established throughout China. Second, new kinds of institutions were needed to finance and manage complex organisations and ensure their profitability, especially those that could not depend on traditional kinship systems. Progress here was desultory and, until the 1930s, there were still loud calls for the Chinese merchant class to emulate British and other modern business structures. But clearly these calls went largely unheeded.

Third, more officials and merchants appreciated the new sciences of business economics derived from British and Japanese practices. Many more had worked in foreign companies and some had studied in American business schools both in China and in the US. They were fully aware of what was needed for them to compete at the highest levels of capitalist enterprise. Officials and merchants as "bourgeois nationalists" spoke of their willingness to cooperate, if not work in tandem, in the interests of both country and enterprises. But the conditions were extraordinarily difficult. On the one hand, foreign enterprises had a head start and remained better organised. On the other, a radical new generation of nationalists was both impatient for dramatic improvements in the country's wealth and power and distrustful of the idea that private profit may be a public good. As idealistic patriots, they often suspected the merchant classes of collaborating with foreign agencies to profit themselves and prevent the economy from prospering for the benefit of the Chinese people.[24]

Nevertheless, the modernisation of a new Chinese merchant class was unmistakable. It had begun in Hong Kong where it found its voice in the writings of Wang Tao (1828–1897) when he brought his ideas with him to Shanghai. Others who had settled in Hong Kong added their voices to what amounted to a call for a patriotic bourgeoisie. This approach was further developed by a class of compradores who also moved from the Hong Kong periphery to the emergent economic centre of Shanghai.[25] The rise of the compradore capitalists brought focus to the question as to how much they had learned from the British merchant houses they worked for.

They were aware that there must be new kinds of officially supported enterprises that would be qualitatively different from the decrepit system that had failed in Canton. But, as they were themselves aware, the component parts of political power and economic risk-taking remained similar. Mandarins would emulate British politicians whom they perceived to have worked closely with successful men who made their fortunes from trade. Given the disadvantageous conditions in China under

the unequal treaties, the mandarins would go further
to supervise active entrepreneurs directly. They offered
protection for these risk-takers so that the entrepreneurs
could compete successfully with the foreign capitalists.
In some cases, retired mandarins became key members
of the enterprises they had helped to form. While they
did not themselves become entrepreneurs, they began
to recognise the advantages in educating their family
members to enter the world of business. This was a
sharp departure from Chinese tradition, in which the
mandarin-scholars were respected but were expected to
despise trade.

There were many-faceted responses to the British
challenge in the China ports, and in Hong Kong and
Malaya (that is, the Malay Peninsula, including Singapore). Here were the trading families on the periphery
of China who mastered modern ideas of production and
marketing. There were two classic examples. The first,
the Oei Tiong Ham companies of the Dutch East Indies
followed European multinational examples, and spread
themselves into British territories as well. The second
were the Zhongshan Cantonese from Sydney who established the Sincere and Wing On department stores in
Hong Kong and Shanghai.[26] They created enterprises
that became models of modern business. Others adapted
quickly to the transport trade, notably venturing into
the cargo shipping business in Australia and Malaya, and
learning to compete with larger British companies in the
region. The shipping operations grew in strength with
wider competitive experiences. They were, together
with other industrial enterprises, specially dynamic in
Shanghai to which were attracted the most enterprising people from neighbouring provinces, if not from all

over the country as well. As they made rapid progress from the late 1920s, they were confronted within the country by civil war and then the Japanese invasion, and externally by the ravages of the Great Depression. When the war ended in 1945, and the victors looked forward to a period of post-war recovery and prosperity, the entrepreneurs in China had little time to recover before the Communists won their decisive victory and began to implement their plans for the nationalisation of all industries. Those who managed to re-locate to Hong Kong were fortunate and had fresh opportunities to start again. They took advantage of the legal freedoms and remarkable opportunities created by the Cold War, and started their new success stories and are continuing to this day.[27]

There were other areas of success. Old-style private banks in Shanghai, Hong Kong and Malaya transformed themselves into modern financial organisations. Although these companies were never able to dominate the financial markets, they grew quickly and were valuable for providing capital for small and medium-sized enterprises. In this way, they created intermediate Chinese informal networks that paralleled the larger ones of the British and filled important niches in regional commerce. These laid the foundations for what came to be seen later as the historical core of "Chinese capitalism". How these networks supplemented the framework of Anglo-American multinationals is being studied today.[28]

Why the adjective "Chinese" to qualify the capitalism that emerged after the 1960s? Many scholars see it as rent-seeking and Yoshihara Kunio has linked it to the "ersatz capitalism" he has found in his notable study of

Southeast Asia.[29] It was recognisably capitalist insofar as
the protagonists institutionalised the use of capital for
profitable ends. But what were the qualities that distinguished this from the capitalism seen as originating
in nineteenth-century London? First, the Chinese who
sought to be industrialists had no secure legal or financial
base on which to build their industries for the long haul.
Where rent-seeking was possible, even readily available,
it was understandable why most of them were tempted
to take the easy way out.

Secondly, there was, and still is, among Chinese a
predisposition to individual and hands-on risk-taking
on behalf of the family, usually with the full backing
of the family. It followed, therefore, that there was always the obligation to meet family expectations and not
to trust people outside. This, in turn, discouraged the
entrepreneurs from building formal systems of management. The owners invariably valued leadership flexibil-
ity and responsibility over managerial efficiency. Many of
their companies have become public ones, but even these
are still controlled by the family. As a result, there were
definite limits to the size of the firm. Traditionally, the
solution was to support the initiative of kinsmen to reach
out and help create a network of related enterprises.
When necessary, the networks were extended to link up
with those more distantly connected. In this way, most
businesses remained family-owned and only minimally
adapted themselves to take advantage of the British laws
and regulatory practices available to them.

The adaptability of these small firms and the speed of
their responses to new opportunities have been much
commented on.[30] Their methods remained viable in
the midst of revolutionary changes, whether in China

or in the region, and, in more recent decades, even in
global business. They still form the backbone of the
SMEs (small and medium-sized enterprises) that the
Chinese overseas networks have made so formidable.
Their success has been due to the narrow definition
of trading that Chinese businessmen have been content
with, one that could not support large industrial organisations and was, therefore, not competitive against
publicly financed multinationals. But their network response helped them to escape the fate of similar family
businesses in Britain and they are agile and reinventable,
as are modern American SMEs. Today, we are inclined
to believe that such adaptable approaches may be well
suited for creative entrepreneurship in the new economy
of the twenty-first century.

This brings me back to the American connection.
The British had laid the foundations in eastern Asia for
an increasingly aggressive challenge by American enterprises in the twentieth century. Here the indirect influences have been particularly fruitful through American
educational institutions. While the Chinese admired the
cultural values and intellectual content of British and
continental universities, the business classes found the
American social science and business school offerings
more directly useful to them. The large numbers of
private missionary colleges in the United States welcoming students from China was a significant factor in their
popularity. At a time when it was already becoming clear
among most Chinese that the English language was winning out as the language of business, this access to tertiary
business training was widely appreciated.[31] It promised
to create an Anglicised class of Chinese functionaries to
serve the China coast communities, but it also inspired

among them the desire and confidence to compete with the established British firms that dominated the region.

Here, too, the Chinese learnt a mixed set of lessons from the Anglo-American experience. It may appear that the main lesson is that free enterprise is best. Among some of the Chinese overseas, notably those in North America and Australasia, that may well have been so. But the more memorable lessons of the past two centuries are all linked to issues pertaining to political power. When the use of such power was benign, as it was for British business in the Treaty Ports and the colonies, trading was predictable. Risks were more easily calculated, errors could be legally rectified, and unwelcome competition discouraged. Chinese entrepreneurs, too, could enjoy the benefits of a supportive officialdom. Two examples, those of Tan Kah Kee (Chen Jiageng) and Li Ka-shing (Li Jiacheng), demonstrate the importance of such symbiotic relationships. They also highlight some of the changes that have occurred between the first and second half of the twentieth century in Anglo-Chinese business relations outside China.

Tan Kah Kee (1874–1961) was a great believer in modern education and is famous for being the first Chinese to found a private modern university in China – this was Xiamen University. His son-in-law, Lee Kong Chian (Li Guangqian, 1894–1967), continued in his footsteps in supporting education and his grandson, Lee Seng Tee (Li Chengzhi), has carried on the family tradition as a benefactor of many institutions in Britain and the United States, including Wolfson College in Cambridge. Tan Kah Kee was spectacularly successful in the plantation business in Malaya. When he started his rubber business at the turn of the century, he received

British appreciation and encouragement. The industry was new and world demand could not be met without bursts of energy that men like Tan Kah Kee could provide. But when restriction schemes were imposed on rubber production in the 1920s in the face of surplus supplies, the Chinese felt they were being discriminated against in favour of British rubber estates. Furthermore, Tan Kah Kee had ventured into industrial production and was seen as directly challenging manufacturing interests in Britain. His business eventually failed. His failure was particularly unfortunate.[32] Although he and his supporters resented the "imperial preference" philosophy that they saw as colonial protectionism, the discriminatory practices were accepted and even shrugged off. Modern capitalism, it was concluded, was bound to national interests, and this was comparable to traditional policies where political power and influence played a powerful role in business. Until the day when Chinese controlled their own politics, trading was a form of learning, and adapting to, new political forces.

For Li Ka-shing, the story was different, although he, too, made a spectacular fortune and founded Shantou University in his home city, Shantou or Swatow, in eastern Guangdong province. He was, in the 1980s, one of the several far-sighted entrepreneurs in Hong Kong. In the eyes of the Chinese, the British were no longer in control of Hong Kong's future by that time. A sign of how things had changed was when Li Ka-shing took over in 1984 the well-established company of Hutchison, one of the most venerable of British hongs. Big players in China were growing in influence, especially following the economic reforms of Deng Xiaoping (1904–1997). Although China was itself a supplicant for foreign skills and investments, its growing presence in the colony was unmistakable. Also, the geopolitics of Sino-American and Sino-Japanese relations had marginalised British interests. With only managerial responsibility and not political dominance, Britain was only one side of a triangular if not quadrilateral power equation. And the Chinese entrepreneurs knew what they had to do to adjust to the changes. For all the praise for genuine capitalist freedom by Milton Friedman and his follow-ers, Hong Kong adjusted to the new power relation-ships. Businessmen like Li Ka-shing understood how much those forces had shifted. The multiple possibili-ties across national borders were matched with the new political alignments. This was not only because Britain was a smaller player, although that was relevant, but also because Sino-American political entanglements, in-cluding those of the Guomindang and Taiwan in Hong Kong, began to affect major business transactions. It is in this context that Li Ka-shing and others could launch their forays into well-established British businesses in the colony.[33]

But Li Ka-shing's activities were only exceptional in limited ways. Although his companies are publicly listed, he remains the dynamic hands-on leader concerned for his family empire. Like most entrepreneurs in Hong Kong, the mainstay of his business has been real es-tate. This is trading in a recognisably traditional form. Chinese confidence and skills in property businesses de-rive from their agrarian respect for land, and records dating back at least two millennia show what their con-cerns have focused on. These skills have spread to every continent where the Chinese have gone. All other busi-nesses were always safer when founded on the bedrock of land ownership. It is remarkable how strongly this principle has been adhered to down the ages and how much it remains one of the pillars of Chinese risk-taking advances. It puts in context the narrow sense of trading that the Chinese have been comfortable with. This may have inhibited them from venturing into the large-scale enterprises that the Anglo-American industrialists and financiers have pioneered, but may still be relevant for the kick-off stage of the new economy that favours dynamic and versatile approaches.

It is in this context that the Chinese have never believed that the British are better than they are in trading. Fighting, yes, for a century or so, but not trading, except that they did learn from the British how much better the British traders fared when they had a supportive government and superior fighting technology behind them. Now those within China are looking outside for the technology and the macroeconomic principles that could make China more prosperous quickly. The Chinese overseas, especially those who do business in the East and Southeast Asian region, seem more ambivalent. Both locally and in their trading relations with China, they recognise the advantages of global trends in cross-border business ties, but they also know that political power remains vital in economic activities.

The state-supervised enterprises in China today may not be able to compete with strong overseas networks, whether Chinese or not. There is a pendulum that swings between excessive public control and too much private sector freedom. For example, the Guomindang businesses that dominated Taiwan for three decades relaxed their controls but did not succumb to pressures for a liberal market system. Although the Guomindang candidate lost the presidential elections in March 2000, the ties between business and politics still remain close and strong. For the Chinese trading in Southeast Asia, the actual relationships between their business and the local civilian and military bureaucracies vary greatly between Malaysia and Singapore and their immediate neighbours, but the connections have never been stronger. Many would see the government-linked companies of Singapore as the latest manifestation of what may still be the most successful formula for state participation.[34] As for Malaysia, the Chinese businessmen, like those in Indonesia, have learnt to weave in and out of the new circles drawn together into the National Alliance (Barisan Nasional). The United Malay National Organisation (UMNO), the country's leading Malay party, has held power since the establishment of the Federation of Malaya in 1948 and controls this Alliance. The Chinese entrepreneurs have had ample time to locate themselves profitably in relation to that political body and all its associated parties.[35]

I shall not speculate as to how Chinese trading networks will evolve as global markets play a bigger part in national economies. The Chinese have been confirmed in their belief that trading can never be a non-political activity. They have seen how the United States Congress voted every year on their trading relations and what political deals have had to be made to get out of the vicious circle that narrow national interest can produce. They will continue to think that each economy will not be free from local power structures, and these in turn are constrained if not determined by elements in history and culture. Modern economic development may modify those structures somewhat, but fundamental changes will need more revolutionary methods and the generations of Chinese today will not be keen to see such revolutions for a long time.

This is not to say that the trading Chinese are too conservative to change. Events in China during the twentieth century have demonstrated that the Chinese can endure and survive the most radical of changes when they have no choice. I certainly do not think that they are waiting for the Anglo-American global influence to retreat so that they can return to their traditional ways. Chinese entrepreneurs, with their deep respect for power concerns, would expect those Anglo pressures on China and the Chinese to continue as long as the United States remains as powerful as it now is. They know these pressures will engender more changes, not only to China itself but also to the Anglo-Chinese relationship.

Though the Chinese believe that they are as good at trading as the British, they will probably acknowledge that British organisations, managerial skills and legal practices have been very helpful as models for them to reengineer better enterprises for the twenty-first century. They will not go back to the old Canton system of state trading, nor will they be content with a modernised form of the English East India Company. But they might well, on top of the well-tried use of informal networks by the Chinese overseas, build not one but many similar East India companies to meet their expanded multiple needs. The current models would also have Japanese and Korean elements that have proven to be successful. The new "Chinese capitalism" may always be a contradiction in terms, but the special mix of public and private in the Chinese trading economy is likely to emerge as a variant of Anglo-American capitalism. The trading British did not set out to teach the Chinese their business. Those who thought they had more than trade to offer were to follow later. Their efforts "to convert" were to meet with unexpected responses, and that will be the subject of the next chapter.

4 "To convert"

The Chinese fought better on land than at sea but they traded well wherever they went. Losing repeatedly to foreigners in all their wars in the nineteenth century was a traumatic experience from which China has yet to recover fully. Learning to trade efficiently in a capitalist system was easier, but the political partners whom Chinese merchants have had both inside and outside the country were difficult to please. When we come to the words, "to convert", however, the picture is different again. Meeting with a powerful and persistent alien religion was an experience the Chinese had not had for a very long time. When Buddhism captured their imagination nearly 2,000 years ago, it brought a spiritual rhetoric that filled their lives and, by enriching the Chinese language as well, stimulated their minds and earned their admiration. Digesting that body of texts and their wealth of ideas for the next millennium seemed to have satisfied most Chinese until recent times.[1] They themselves remained without an indigenous tradition of religious conversion. Chinese elites felt a duty to bring their civilisation to non-Han minorities from time to time, but the idea of converting others to a Chinese religion was not something they readily understood. It is interesting to note that China, apart from some pantheistic beliefs, did not develop a religion of its own. This is unusual for a continuous historic civilisation. Most Chinese seemed content to combine imported Buddhism with indigenous practices until Confucianism was formalised into an imperial philosophy to regulate civic lives. For them, the most permanent consequence of the "Buddhist conquest", besides the religion itself, was its impact on the Chinese language and art and, consequently, the people's thought patterns. That impact provided a useful indication of the complex process of conversion, and it is one of the themes that I shall pursue in this chapter.

When Arthur Waley used the word "convert", he was primarily thinking of the generations of missionaries who had left home to devote themselves to the Christianisation of the Chinese. One immediately thinks of pioneers like Robert Morrison (1782–1834), who went to Malacca early in the nineteenth century and waited there for the opening of China. His early converts there, and in Hong Kong, helped bring Christian tracts to Hong Xiuquan (1813–1864), self-proclaimed brother of Jesus Christ and the founder of the Taiping Heavenly Kingdom. But the violent consequences of that rebellion did little to enhance the status of the religion in Chinese eyes, least of all among the mandarins and the local literati families who suffered most from that murderous sweep across half the empire. Although later missionaries did distance themselves from that unfortunate start with Hong Xiuquan, their task was thereafter uphill all the way. They met with suspicion almost everywhere. Some of them, as well as their converts, were attacked or killed by local Chinese and, almost invariably, such attacks and killings were followed by armed retribution by British and French troops. And those, in turn, were followed by increased hostility towards all efforts at preaching and conversion.[2]

It was not surprising that, eventually, actual prose-lytising was subordinated to a service approach through building and staffing hospitals and schools. Even these were not always welcome. A few exceptional mission-ary scholars writing in English did make a small impres-sion among the elites. For example, someone like James Legge (1814–1897), who translated the Chinese classics, and Young J. Allen (1836–1907), who established news-papers like *Wanguo gongbao* (Chinese Globe Magazine, 1868–1883, and *A Review of the Times*, 1889–1907) in Shanghai. Others were men like John Fryer (1839–1928) and W. A. P. Martin (1827–1916), who worked at the Interpreters' College (Tongwen Guan, established in 1862), the institution that organised systematic trans-lations of works of modern mathematics, science, law, geography and world history into Chinese.[3] From 1860 to the turn of the century, some 350 texts were translated from English, many of these done by men of the cloth and as many of them American as British. It looked as if, where religious conversion might have been prema-ture, a different kind of conversion, achieved by making books on secular subjects available, would have to do.

In contrast, the Japanese, who humiliated the Chinese in the 1894–1895 war, were surprisingly well received after the war. From the publication of the research of Saneto Keishu (1896–1985) in 1939–1940, we know how much Japanese teachers and educational officials contributed to the modernisation of China from the late 1890s to the establishment of the Republic in 1912.[4] Douglas Reynolds, in his fine study of the Xinzheng or New Systems Revolution, went so far as to call this period "the golden decade" of Sino-Japanese relations. This could be seen as the time when the Japanese returned their cultural debt to the Chinese by hastening the introduction of Western knowledge to China through the innumerable translations from Western languages that they had done for themselves for decades. Compared with those translated from the English before 1900, the number of books translated from the Japanese in one decade, 1900–1910, was more than one and a half times all those done by the various official translation bureaus during the 40 years before.[5]

In neither case was there any question of religious conversion. For the English translators, they had learnt to steer studiously clear of works specifically extolling the Christian faith. For those translating from the Japanese, the rhetoric of a common respect for Confucianism eased the transfer of both knowledge and ideas. For one short moment in history, the Japanese provided a short cut to modern knowledge that the awakened Chinese elites were willing to embrace enthusiastically. This was not simply asking the Japanese to help implement the old way of "using the foreigners' ways to defend against the foreigners" (*yiyi zhiyi*).[6] There was a genuine realisation, confirmed by Japanese educational successes and reconfirmed by Japanese victory in the Russo-Japanese War, that the new learning promised a long-term progress to the future which China desperately needed if it was to save itself and its civilisation.

The Sino-Japanese War of 1894–1895 opened the Chinese mind to the breakthrough the empire really needed. The last of a series of defeats by superior naval forces, it drove the Chinese to seek knowledge from the West with a new thoroughness, via what was more accessible in Japanese translation. It is now clear that the highest Japanese authorities approved plans to engage the Chinese in an enterprise to drive the West out of the region. Had that been a genuine effort at cooperation, the Chinese might have been proud to remember that "golden decade". Unfortunately, real Japanese intentions were exposed by their plans to annex the Korean peninsula in stages between 1905 and 1910. At the onset of the First World War, its imperial plans were further revealed when Japan made its infamous Twenty-one Demands of 1915, and followed that by replacing Germany as the dominant power in Shandong province.[7] As a result, most of the thousands of students still studying in Japan decided they had to leave, and China was happy thereafter to forget that it ever owed Japan anything.

Let me make two points here in the context of conversion. The first is that Japan's extraordinary influence on China's attitudes towards modernity was a kind of conversion. Great claims have been made about the way the Japanese translations impacted on a whole generation of young Chinese who not only learnt of the West through them but also adopted the vocabulary the Japanese used to convey the new ideas that were introduced. There is no doubt about the linguistic influence, especially in the new schools built all over the empire, which used textbooks translated from the Japanese.[8] But this should not be confused with acceptance of the content. The new ideas had originated from the West and the most important of these were largely made available through works translated into Japanese from the English. But it was the half-century from the 1850s which laid the foundations for the modern ideas circulating in the Treaty Ports. The works translated directly from English into Chinese during that period had already begun to open the eyes of the leading mandarins at the court.

The return of the brightest young officials and students from Britain and the United States and the most successful among the overseas Chinese had further prepared the ground for change. Men like Yan Fu (1854–1921) and Lin Shu (1852–1924), who translated some of the philosophical and literary classics of the British, were no less influential than Liang Qichao (1873–1929) and others who did their translations from the Japanese. In addition, there were others like Sun Yat-sen who turned new words into slogans and political ideas into action. Certainly, a greater number of indirect translations were made, but the desire and will to learn, through translations from the English in particular, were already there. The threat by the imperialist powers for several years after 1898 to "carve up the Chinese melon" had become a fearful probability. The dramatic acts following the so-called Hundred Days' Reform the same year, and the Boxer catastrophe in 1899–1900, merely added a greater sense of urgency and spurred more of the young to challenge the orthodox views of their elders.[9] The wider impact of these events can be seen in the debates conducted in Hong Kong and the Straits Settlements among the Chinese there. Those debates held in English reflected the extent to which British political rhetoric had been internalised. The best example of this may be found in Lim Boon Keng's (Lin Wenqing, 1869–1957) essays, collected in the volume *The Chinese Crisis from Within* (1901).[10] He was a peripheral figure for Chinese intellectuals in Shanghai and other cities in China, who were unlikely to have read the book, but the English terms he used pointed to the kind of terms that were also being powerfully employed in contemporary writings in Chinese.

The second point is, with the willingness to convert at this level, why turn to the Japanese and not learn more directly from English-language original writings? After all, dedicated people like W. A. P. Martin, Young J. Allen, John Fryer, Gilbert Reid (1857–1927) and Timothy Richard (1845–1919) had been working for decades to make works relating to science, industry, history, politics and geography available to younger Chinese.[11] Many senior officials and budding examination candidates found the works exciting. The Japanese links with Confucianism and the British and Americans with Christianity meant that only the latter were associated with a kind of conversion that implied rejection of Chinese tradition.

At the same time, a secular conversion did take place in the years 1901–1910. Although using the same word "conversion", I suggest that this latter conversion required no less a change of mindset than the idea of a religious conversion. And, if we recognise that the secular change had begun with some key Chinese thinkers decades earlier than the Japanese impact in 1900–1910, it was the English-language-based aids to that conversion that enabled the Chinese to appreciate so quickly what the Japanese short-cuts had to offer.

Nevertheless, to what the Chinese people should convert was still unclear. The majority of the literati class were confident that Chinese learning remained the basic principle and conversion should only be to things of practical utility, as suggested by the famous phrase of Viceroy Zhang Zhidong, "Chinese learning as foundation, Western learning for application". Let me point to some examples from the era of the New Systems Revolution, roughly the last decade of Zhang Zhidong's long and distinguished life. In 1906, the scholar-archaeologist and novelist Liu E (1857–1909) published the novel, *Lao Can youji*, or the story of Lao Can's travels. In it, he tells us of a dream about the sea off the coast of Shandong, not far from where the Japanese navy had inflicted defeats on the Chinese eleven years earlier, in 1895. This was close to the port of Weihaiwei, which the British leased in 1898 together with Kowloon in the frenzy of "melon-carving" a few months after the xenophobic Boxers in Shandong began to attract attention. In the dream, the narrator saw a wounded ship heading to shore with its passengers. But instead of saving the passengers, the crew proceeded to rob them. Liu E used the image to describe the declining Qing empire in which the Chinese people were victimised beyond endurance. But he personally expected the Qing dynasty to recover and still put his faith in China's superior traditions that, although much neglected in practice, retained the vitality to restore China to greatness. He saw no future for radical reformers and revolutionaries, whom he compared to the rapacious crew taking advantage of helpless passengers. He had no reason to place any faith in the religious and secular ideas brought to China by the British, whether directly or via the Japanese.[12]

Liu E's hometown was Dantu (Chinkiang, or Zhenjiang, not far from Shanghai and itself a Treaty Port in Liu E's lifetime). His novel has become a classic. If it were compared with two other classics of the same period from the same town, a similar faith in tradition may also be found. The two are the *Baiyuzhai cihua*, by my grandmother's father, Chen Tingzhuo (1853–92) and the *Songren yishi huibian*, by my mother's cousin, Ding Chuanjing (1870–1930).[13] The first was an insightful study on the *Ci*-poets of the past thousand years, and the second a wonderful collection of anecdotes about personalities of the Song dynasty. Both were wholly devoid of any external influences. Chen, who was about the same age as Liu E, completed his book in 1891, while Ding, who was 13 years younger, published his book just two years after *Lao Can's Travels* appeared, that is, in 1908. What all three had in common was confidence in the permanence of transmitted traditions. All three showed not a whiff of the radical change that was soon to take place a decade later. The anxious voices of the reformers and revolutionaries of their time were hardly representative of the elites of this generation, for the views of these three men were closer to the norm.

What is striking about these men was that their city of Zhenjiang had been a Treaty Port since the 1860s. All had lived for 30 or 40 years within sight of British and American missions before they wrote their books, but only Liu E gave any hint of awareness that powerful new ideas of a dominant foreign power like Britain had been introduced into China. In recent decades, most works of history concentrate on the men who were excited by the challenge of new ideas. The fact was, the men mentioned above ignored those challenges and were far more representative of the majority of literati in their faith in Chinese tradition. All were hostile to the idea that spiritual agents sent from the English-speaking world could have anything to offer them. Yet, within a decade of Ding Chuanjing's collection of Song dynasty anecdotes in 1908, a rush of intellectual and cultural conversions began swiftly to crowd people like them off centre-stage altogether.[14]

There was a huge jump in "conversions" by the end of the First World War, but few of them were to Christianity. What, then, was it that converted young educated Chinese in large numbers? Bearing in mind that thousands of dedicated British missionaries like Robert Morrison had been working with young Chinese in Malacca and Hong Kong for more that 80 years, it is surprising how few converts they made before 1918. The China Inland Mission alone, led by James Hudson Taylor (1832–1905), had sent 800 or so missionaries, and Timothy Richard and his colleagues inducted a new generation of Chinese into modern learning through the Guangxue hui (The Society for the Diffusion of Christian and General Knowledge, founded in 1887).[15] Many of them had played down religious teaching, and the secular knowledge they provided met Chinese intellectual curiosity and was clearly better received. Also, the cooperation between British and American missionaries reaped their best fruit in the many colleges and hospitals they founded. The Americans in particular were keen to send their converts back to the United States for further training, and some of these converts continued with Christian work all their lives. Whether or not the input of capital and massive human energy in these efforts was commensurate with the numbers of Chinese actually converted is debatable. It is enough to note that the push to bring modern schooling to most corners of the country within a decade of the foundation of the Republic in 1911 had begun with Christian missionaries. And this contrasted greatly with the minimal Chinese official resources put into the drive for secular education at the turn of the century.[16]

From time to time, we are reminded that Sun Yat-sen had been converted to Christianity, that his successor as leader of the Guomindang, Chiang Kai-shek, had also converted to Methodism when he married Sun's sister-in-law, Soong Mei-ling. What is less emphasised are Sun Yat-sen's early contacts with a series of British teachers from Iolani College in Honolulu and Government Central School in Hong Kong (later, Queen's College). He then went to the Chinese College of Medicine founded by Ho Kai (He Qi, 1859–1914), a devout Christian convert who married an English wife. There he established a close and lasting relationship with his teacher, Dr James Cantlie (1851–1926). The cumulative influences of all these men on Sun Yat-sen had been deep, but more important than his Christianity was his secular conversion to modernity as the saviour of China. His new religion was the idea of *guojia* or patria, of nationalism and national salvation through revolution.[17] For many Chinese of his generation, Christianity was a symbol not of rejection of tradition but of discovery and progress. And underlying that progress was the power of the scientific knowledge he received in his schools.

This response was also found among the sojourning Chinese in British Malaya, where officials established a few secular government schools but were reluctant to promote Christianity in a tolerant plural society whose development they wished to encourage. Of the various missionaries who established schools in the major towns, the British were often the minority among strong contingents of protestant Americans and Catholics from Ireland and continental Europe. The Chinese studied together with the children of immigrants from British India and Ceylon or Sri Lanka (a mixture of Hindus and Muslims, mainly from the south), local Eurasians and

Muslims from the various Malay states. Their teachers were often recruited from among local Christian converts or Christians directly from South Asia and southern China. Again, although most students accepted the British worldview and went on to serve the local government and businesses, actual converts to Christianity among the Chinese were never many.

In sharp contrast, the drive for Chinese schools teaching the Chinese national language and modern science, and using textbooks published in Shanghai, was irresistible.[18] Here different kinds of conversion were experienced. These "conversions" may have been indirect, but they were deep and led to serious challenges to perspectives on how the local Chinese were expected to behave in British-administered territories, notably those civic values highlighted in the officially approved texts used in the English-language schools. What was interesting was that modern ideas were not always acceptable when coming from Anglo teachers themselves, but were much better received when filtered through Chinese-language books written by modernising Chinese in China.

I have suggested earlier that different groups of Chinese responded to British culture differently, but wonderment at spectacular technological advances led to the first converts. Eventually, the acceptance of the underlying scientific principles that needed to be mastered transformed the nature of education for all. There was nothing smooth or natural about such processes of conversion to foreign ways, especially to foreign ideas. The impact of British and other Western ideas, no less than the Chinese response to them, was erratic and unpredictable. However powerful these ideas were when they first appeared among the Chinese, the Chinese ultimately picked only what they wanted, what they thought they most urgently needed. Does such a rational process qualify as conversion? It may not have been a religious experience, but the word is the most apt for describing what happened to the Chinese in the way they thought about the world. I hasten to add that this did not mean that they agreed with the British and adopted their values. What changed was the capacity to use the Chinese equivalents of modern terms to further absorb the latest knowledge and methods that the Western world had to offer and, where necessary, to counter the criticisms and attacks by foreigners on what the Chinese believed was their due.

The increasing use of the vernacular language (*baihua*), also *guoyu* (national language) or Mandarin, and now called *putonghua* or the common language, early in the twentieth century, is a useful index of conversion. Better known as a literary revolution, the Baihuawen Movement led by Chen Duxiu (1879–1942), who had studied in Japan, and Hu Shi (1891–1962), educated in the United States, was a liberating experience. It freed young Chinese from the straitjacket of both classical sentence forms and the officialese in which all public documents and correspondence were written. The classical language had been steadily loosened by popular Buddhist teaching and story-telling, and the writing of novels like Journey to the West (*Xiyou ji*), The Water Margin (*Shuihu zhuan*), and the Dream of the Red Chamber (*Honglou meng*), over several centuries. At the beginning of the twentieth century, Lin Shu still insisted on translating Shakespeare and several English novelists into classical Chinese. The popularity of his work may have helped to slow down the enthusiastic embrace of *baihua*, but the style and quality of his writings introduced a new literary sensibility to a new

generation of Chinese.[19] These contributed to the at-
traction of literary and artistic values from the English
romantics, the free and rumbustious prose of Charles
Dickens and even the gloomy morality tales of Thomas
Hardy. I need not dwell on those young scholars who
were stimulated by study in, or visits to, Britain: poets
like Xu Zhimo (1895–1931) and the philosopher of
aesthetics, Zhu Guangqian (1897–1986), novelists like
Lao She (1899–1966) and Xu Dishan (1893–1941)
and, among others, the close friend of E. M. Forster's,
the journalist Xiao Qian (Hsiao Ch'ien, 1910–1999).[20]
They each added to an awareness of another Britain,
one of sensitivity and spiritual enlightenment that the
Chinese people would not have found in the Chinese
books and essays about the British at that time. I shall say
a little more about three very different men: Zhu, Xu and
Xiao.

Zhu Guangqian deserves a mention as an example
of a twofold, direct and indirect, beneficiary of British
education. He came from a family of distinguished
Confucian scholars and had negligible English when
he was sent on a scholarship from China in 1918 to
the University of Hong Kong. Through his teachers in
English literature, psychology and education, he was introduced to the English literary classics and the works of
Plato and Aristotle. He was thus "converted", so thoroughly that, after graduation in 1923, he sought to study
directly in Britain (1925–1929, and then spent another
four years in Europe). He received his doctorate at the
University of Glasgow and expanded his thesis for publication as *The Psychology of Tragedy: a critical study of various
theories of tragic pleasure*. He went on to become the doyen
of literary theory scholars in China. To capture the way

he saw his moment of "conversion", let me quote from his essay of 1944, when he recalls his professor at Hong Kong University:

> ...[You are] my spiritual wet nurse. I learnt English poetry from you. The first poem you asked me to read was The Rime of the Ancient Mariner. When I first read it, I found the story of the old sailor shooting the albatross so dry and dull, and laughable. But after you guided me through the poem again, the syllables and imagery were so beautiful, the alternating arrangements so finely placed. Only an artist can touch up an ordinary world to look like a beautiful one, only a skilled teacher can open up an apparently ordinary world to reveal the beauty brewing inside. You once made for me this kind of miracle.[21]

And, indeed, this miracle led him thereafter to share his excitement over new ideas about literature with generations of students. He not only became a dedicated teacher, but through a prose that was fresh and free, he inspired them, beginning with the "Twelve Letters to the Young" he wrote from Glasgow in 1926.[22] It was this language of poetry that served as the bedrock of the educational psychology and philosophy of aesthetics that he wrote on throughout his long and fruitful life. This may not have been quite the conversion Christian missionaries had wanted, but the idealism Zhu Guangqian sought to convey was no less a deep change in mindset, perhaps the next best thing.

Since I started with Arthur Waley's essay on "A Debt to China" and am speaking in Cambridge, I would also like to mention Xu Zhimo, the poet Waley wrote about, who came to King's College at the recommendation of

Goldsworthy Lowes Dickinson (1862–1932). In Waley's words,

> Never has anyone belonged more wholly and sincerely to the Romantic Period. Byron was his model and hero. He loved to think of himself as the Chinese Childe Harold, though nature has scarcely fitted him for that part. There was nothing Byronic about his long thin face, with the stubborn mouth that seemed to express, above all, the determination to lead his own life in his own way; he had not a particle of Byronic cynicism.[23]

Waley regretfully says, "Great Englishmen had lived in China before, but failed to make any impression on the Chinese intelligentsia". He saw that men like Lowes Dickinson (1862–1932), Bertrand Russell (1872–1970) and Robert Trevelyan (1872–1951), who went to China to make friends and learn, "gave the Chinese a completely new view of us". I am not sure that that was really so. Lowes Dickinson's views on the ancient Greeks did become available in Chinese and some of Robert Trevelyan's translations of Greek tragedies were known, but we have no record of their influence on the Chinese they met.[24] Bertrand Russell, however, was a world figure whom the Chinese intellectual world was keen to listen to when he was invited to visit China in 1920. But he turned out to be a puzzle and a disappointment to his hosts. They began by lionising him, but his frank and uncompromising views at a time of nationalist enthusiasm and naive discovery of Russian socialism were presented at a wrong time and place. Thus, he left only a minimal impact on his audiences. His remarkable effort to explain China, *The Problem of China*, published in 1922, was ignored and not translated until 1996 and, till this day, there is still a slight sense of regret among some older Chinese that the early contact had not been more fruitful.[25]

With Waley's thought in mind, allow me to indulge myself with one more quote, from the subject of Waley's essay, Xu Zhimo, the first truly modern poet of China. The poem captures something of what might have been had there indeed been more opportunities for the gentler folk of both countries to meet, instead of the usual list of officials, merchants and soldiers. I quote a few lines, from a translation of his "Second Farewell to Cambridge":

> Quietly I am leaving
> Just as quietly I came ...
>
> In search of a dream? You pole a tiny boat
> Toward where the green is even more green
> To collect a load of stars, as songs
> Rise in the gleaming stellar light.
> But to-night my voice fails me;
> Silence is the best tune of farewell;
> Even crickets are still for me,
> And still is Cambridge tonight.
>
> Silently I am going
> As silently I came;
> I shake my sleeves,
> Not to bring away a patch of cloud.[26]

Here the Chinese language is wholly freed.

About fifteen years later, in 1942, with the help of E. M. Forster (1879–1970), Xiao Qian (Hsiao Ch'ien) gave up his lectureship at the School of Oriental and African Studies (SOAS) in London to study at King's College, Cambridge.[27] Born in Beijing in a part-Mongol family, Xiao was orphaned at a young age. The American wife of a cousin helped him get to a Presbyterian school where he learnt his English early. Faced with a joyless fundamentalist Christianity, his later "conversion" after attending a Catholic (Furen) University and then graduating from a Protestant (Yenching) one, was to the English novel, first the Victorians and then modern writers: D. H. Lawrence, Virginia Woolf, E. M. Forster and James Joyce. He began to translate poems and stories from the English and then translated Chinese writings, including some new Chinese plays, into English. He also began to write his own stories. But, in the end, he was drawn to study with Edgar Snow at the School of Journalism at Yenching University and went to work for the best-known independent newspaper of its time, the *Dagongbao* of Tianjin. From there he went to SOAS in 1939. One of the very few Chinese in England during the war, he taught Chinese, lectured to pro-China societies, broadcast for the BBC, and published several books, including *A Harp with a Thousand Strings*, where Waley's radio talk, "A Debt to China" was reprinted.

As Xiao Qian recalls in his autobiography:

> I met many British authors through the PEN meetings... My one true friendship was with Forster. Our friendship was not really so surprising... The best friend in Forster's life, and the one who most profoundly influenced him, was Goldsworthy Lowes Dickinson, whose biography Forster wrote. [Dickinson] wrote *Letters from John Chinaman*, in which he described China as a utopia in order to satirize Britain. It was because of this book, and his friendship with Dickinson, that Forster conceived a passionate interest in the East.[28]

Xiao and Forster exchanged over eighty letters, of which forty have survived. Xiao concludes, "Thus did a young Chinese literature student come to be friends with a distinguished British author. The author deepened the young man's understanding of Western culture, and the youth added to the author's knowledge of China".[29] That friendship may have been an added reason why Waley thought of those English who could make friends and learn, and give the Chinese "a completely new view of us".

Xiao the patriot returned to China and chose to support Mao Zedong's revolution. When he was persecuted for his bourgeois views in 1957, this was a severe test of his "conversion". But he kept faith and, by the time he was rehabilitated in 1979, he had returned to the English novel. Through Forster's influence, he began with Henry Fielding (1707–1754) and translated *The Life of Jonathan Wild* and then *The History of Tom Jones*. But he never forgot Forster's praise for Joyce's *A Portrait of the Artist as a Young Man* and the critical essay he wrote and read to his learned tutor, George Rylands (1902–1999), on *Finnegans Wake*. In disgrace, his youthful "conversion" led him to begin his masterly and prize-winning translation of *Ulysses* into Chinese. It was finally published in three volumes in 1994, when he was 84 years old.[30]

Zhu Guangqian, Xu Zhimo, and Xiao Qian, like Hu Shi before them, were "converted" through literature in English, especially the language of poetry that Xu Zhimo transmuted into a fresh poetic idiom in Chinese. This may be compared to literary giants in British India like Rabindranath Tagore (1861–1941) and Muhammed Iqbal (1877–1938), whose contacts with English writing

and ideas led them to a vivified poetry in Bengali
and Persian and Urdu respectively. It was, however, a
different situation where students of English did not
write in their mother tongue. Outside China, where
Chinese who were born and had settled in British territories were taught directly by their teachers to write in
English, there was no similar development or impact.
It was only decades later, during the 1950s, that writers of Chinese descent in the Commonwealth began to
make their mark writing in English. About that time,
all around the Commonwealth, writers of Asian and
African descent found their English voices in poetry,
fiction and drama as well as other branches of the fine
arts. Soon after, Asian Americans in the United States,
with a strong contingent among them of Chinese descent, sought to join the English literature mainstream.[31]
But this was a different phenomenon from the kind of
"conversion" that brought a totally new life to literature
in Chinese.

I spoke earlier of the linguistic conversion that became
complete when the vernacular became the language of
all teaching. This impact is not unlike that of Chaucer
using English for his *Canterbury Tales*. Using *baihua* at the
university level to teach every modern subject ensured
an enormous impact on young minds. I have already
mentioned the many liberal arts colleges and universities started in China by the Americans which enshrined
English as the first foreign language in China. There was
strong competition from Japanese and French. Together,
the three languages helped to transform the Chinese
vernacular into a powerful tool with a rich vocabulary
that could transmit all the fresh ideas and discoveries the
people might want from the West.

This linguistic impact rarely came from those who actually used the English language, but there were interesting exceptions from earlier times when most Chinese were still fully confident of the greatness of Chinese civilisation. The first Chinese to master English, who was nevertheless able to remain influential among the Chinese in China, was Yung Wing (Rong Hong, 1828–1912), who went to the United States in 1847 after studies in Hong Kong and graduated from Yale University in 1854. His was a practical English coloured by his Christian faith, but he continued to make contributions to his country's welfare in the field of foreign affairs. Later, many others followed his footsteps, and most of those who also had a good knowledge of classical Chinese repeated his Sino-American career path.[32]

The first person to study at a British university, however, had very different experiences. In his case, he learnt his English from when he was young without having any knowledge of Chinese. This was Ku Hung-ming (Gu Hongming, 1857–1928) of Penang who, after he settled in Beijing as Professor of Latin at Peking University, became the most accessible Chinese for Western visitors to China during the first quarter of the twentieth century. His family had settled in the Malay States, and then the Straits Settlements, for three generations. His foster father, a Scotsman, sent him to school in Scotland about 1870 and he graduated from the University of Edinburgh in 1877. Later colonial Chinese who went to Britain from Malaya and Hong Kong mostly chose to study medicine and law, but Ku Hung-ming took an arts degree, adding to his knowledge of Greek, Latin and German an admiration of the English romantics. On his return to Asia, he experienced a reverse "conversion", falling in love with classical Chinese at a time when the classical scholars mentioned above, like Liu E, Chen Tingzhuo and Ding Chuanjing of Zhenjiang, were all confident of the viability of the civilisation.

Ku Hung-ming may be compared with Lim Boon Keng (Lin Wenqing), another Straits-born English-educated, who had followed him to Edinburgh in 1887. Lim Boon Keng, too, returned to the Chinese classics and also became a strong advocate for the restoration of Confucian values. The "reverse conversion" of both Ku Hung-ming and Lim Boon Keng from an English-based education back into the China fold was the last of its kind.[33] The act of using a foreign language to revive a Chinese faith was repudiated by their compatriots in their lifetime. For most young Chinese, it was the rejuvenated literary works in Chinese by the next generation of writers, like Zhu Guangqian, Xu Zhimo and hundreds of others, that marked the cultural life and style that replaced it.

Religion in China was built on a tradition of inclusiveness. As a result, in all its long history, China has not known wars of religion. By the end of the Song dynasty in the thirteenth century, its people had integrated Buddhist and Taoist ideas into a revived Confucianism. This seems to have removed the need for other faiths and philosophies, but it also enabled most Chinese people to deal with a wide range of religious experiences without trauma or conversions. The existence of an agrarian communitarianism and an imperial orthodoxy was widely accepted. Three stages of living that encouraged social stability and recognised personal development were rationalised to satisfy the members of the elite. The young were exhorted to study and prepare themselves to be Confucian, giving emphasis to moral character through self-cultivation. After middle age, they were encouraged to seek good health and physical resuscitation through select Taoist practices, and this was to be followed by a tranquil old age to which the Buddhist sutras had much to contribute. What need was there for the enthusiasm and excitement of conversion?

When this all-embracing Confucianism that supported the two religions was rejected by the young after the 1920s, following the many calls for revolution, what could be the modern equivalents to replace the traditional three stages? With the conversion to a freer language that carried the new truths of science, embodied in spectacular new technology and reinforced by fierce debates about the supreme faith in "scientism", the young looked for a secular faith. Some found it by committing themselves to nationalist calls to wealth and power. Others were enjoined to "make revolution" by studying science and seeking their fulfilment through social dedication. Here the English-language contribution from the late nineteenth century may clearly be seen.

The Chinese themselves, for example men like Yan Fu, made a difference. Yan Fu had studied science and navigation in the Fuzhou Naval Academy and was among the first to be sent to England to learn the secret of British military power at Greenwich Naval College. I shall come back to him in the next chapter to discuss his qualified admiration of British institutions of governance. His importance here comes from his translations of books by Thomas Huxley and Herbert Spencer, Adam Smith and John Stuart Mill and, most of all, his introduction of Spencer's social Darwinism to several generations of young Chinese.[34] A better-trained scientist was the geologist Ding Wenjiang (1887–1936), who had studied in Glasgow and lived in Britain for seven years. His defence of science provided a major manifesto in refutation of all efforts at restoring traditional Confucian learning, although he also contributed to a growing uncritical faith in the wondrous powers of science. It did not take long for everything scientific to be right and the word "unscientific" to be the strongest dismissal of any argument.[35]

Here the missionaries who sought religious converts had also made a contribution. In their critiques of Chinese religious practices, they introduced the idea of superstition, and the word was translated as *mixin*, or blind faith. *Mixin* became the word that was applied to the practices of astrologers, fortune-tellers and geomancers, as well as the popular beliefs by most Chinese in devils, ghosts and evil spirits. Since all these practices and beliefs were also not accepted by rational Confucians and Buddhists, this powerful word came quickly into common use among the younger generation of educated Chinese. No one expected, however, that it would also become the opposite of the word *kexue*, or scientific, and that it would one day be used against all ideas and values that could be described as "traditional", and also, ironically, against all religions, including Christianity itself. Once *mixin* was embedded in the language as a term of condemnation, with *kexue* or science as the only judge of truth, we have observed something akin to a conversion, a total acceptance of the secular worldview based on reason and observation, on mathematical calculation and laboratory experiment.

This leads me to two of the most remarkable stories that linked China to Britain. It could only have happened in the context of the worship of science and, therefore, could only have happened after the victory of those who believed that they had found a scientific way to rebuild China. There is no need here to dwell on the capabilities of the young Chinese scientists after the Second World War who have won Nobel Prizes through their research done in the other major English-speaking country, the United States. They are but the tip of a growing body of science talent from Asia, mainly China and India, whose achievements outside their countries of origin have dazzled the world. Most of these, however, are virtuoso performances with American and European scientists that tell us little about the impact of science among their peoples at home. The stories that are more revealing are those pertaining to the new faith in "scientific socialism" and a deeper curiosity about the scientific achievements of Chinese civilisation.

The first secretary-general of the Chinese Communist Party, Chen Duxiu, had extolled the young to look to "science and democracy" to save China. In one generation, the rhetoric of "scientific socialism" had entered the nationalist discourse and the debate it engendered threatened to rewrite the social and economic history of China.[36] I do not want to make too much of the fact that the language of capitalism, imperialism and socialism was drawn from the writings of Karl Marx and Friedrich Engels, ultimately from ideas that had been crystallised in the British Museum and had been inspired by the industrial achievements of Manchester. But this may be taken together with the picture of a Britain transformed by the industrial revolution, best represented by several novels of Charles Dickens made popular through the elegant translations by Lin Shu. Through them, the language and the images of an exploitative capitalism made a powerful impact and reinforced the value of science and scientific study. It led to debates about how the seeds of capitalism could be found in the late Ming and early Qing period (sixteenth–seventeenth centuries),[37] and also to the early history of science in traditional China. This was a subject the Chinese themselves had never really appreciated before the advent of modern science. The Chinese were great inventors but did not place much value on the inventors themselves. The name of the inventor of paper was known, so were those of the first great physician and the discoverer of the south-pointing magnetic mechanism, but no one could recall who had invented printing or gunpowder. There was greater appreciation, during the Song, Yuan and Ming dynasties, of the great books on agriculture, sericulture, and materia medica. And, by the eighteenth century, the work of Song Yingxing (b. 1587) on the practical arts, the *Tiangong kaiwu* first published in 1637, had become well respected, notably in Japan, but the idea that there was science behind all the technology and that this science was the key to greater truths and the mastery of nature was strikingly absent.[38]

The awakening among the Chinese scholars began in the 1920s and 1930s. The new interest was hesitant, even apologetic, and no one was confident to make bold scientific claims. But the first steps were taken, notably in their writings on the early history of mathematics, astronomy and geography. They were followed by efforts to link alchemical practices to the origins of chemistry and ancient mechanical devices to modern engineering developments.[39] One of the more ambitious books was the work of two men trained in British medical schools, one in Hong Kong and the other in Cambridge. I refer to the work of Wong Chimin and Ng Lean Tuck (Wu Liande, 1879–1960) who published the *History of Chinese Medicine*, in 1936. Wong Chimin from Hong Kong wrote the historical part, while Ng Lean Tuck, another Queen's Scholar from Malaya, dealt with the new developments in China to which he had made a contribution. This book concentrated on medical happenings from ancient times to the 1930s. It was a useful attempt to link past and present, but the gap between Chinese tradition and modern practice was glaringly large. Neither author did more than note the unbridgeable differences.[40]

About the same time, some students had come to Cambridge to study with Joseph Needham (1900–1995) and planted a seed in his restless and curious mind. This was followed by an opportunity for Needham to go to China during the war to follow up the work being done by British-trained scientists who had returned to China. A series of fruitful meetings with scholars from just about every relevant discipline led to the decision to study the history of science in China. There was no one better to lead this research than Needham himself. Thus began one of the most spectacular voyages of discovery in Anglo-Chinese history, one of which Cambridge University should rightly be proud. Without the conversion to the new faith in science in both its natural and social forms, there would not have been the readiness to give Needham the support and respect that he deserved. It is an extraordinary contribution that has earned him a place in the history of Anglo-Chinese encounters. Bear in mind that the backdrop is the conversion that the British missionaries had failed to achieve, which British science has now succeeded in bringing about. The project to find "A Science Civilisation for China", yet to be completed, has been worthy of the volumes devoted to it. I offer here but a brief personal appreciation of this climax of 150 years of a complex culture-contact.

Joseph Needham did more than anyone to try to discover every bit of science and technology he could find in all the Chinese texts still available, and these have been extensively examined and interpreted in the volumes of *Science and Civilisation in China* published so far. He has contributed to building Chinese national pride and a new sense of direction in modern scholarship about Chinese civilisation. He restored pride to a generation in China which had accepted Chinese "backwardness" as a given – the result of political weakness and cultural stagnation and decay – in a China which it was thought that only modern science could save.

He believed that civilisation was a product of millennia of human effort, and all peoples and areas of the world had contributed to scientific progress. The eventual rise of modern science in Europe was the result of many streams and tributaries flowing into it from many other parts of the world. The varieties of premodern or proto-science show that a science civilisation could have existed prior to the explosive developments of the past three centuries. This is not to say that Chinese civilisation was indisputably a scientific one. But Needham's work suggests that, in the world of the natural sciences, it is conceivable for all past civilisations to become one global civilisation.

I shall not deal with Needham's thoughts on Chinese civilisation. He clearly thought that its philosophy was holistic and organismic and discouraged analytical thought, that the authoritarianism of both the family and state systems limited knowledge collaboration and "technology transfer", and that its examination-based bureaucracy looked down on the discoveries of peasants and artisans. These were relevant factors in China's so-called scientific "inertia" or "stagnation". Of course, we now know that there were numerous texts offering solutions in mathematics, astronomical observations and calculations, agricultural tools and techniques, alchemical "experiments", the discovery of gunpowder, the development of printing, mechanisms in the "heavenly clock". Nevertheless, his question, "Why did China not develop modern science?", was worth asking because it refined the concept of science for different periods of history and revealed the richness of phenomena that have illuminated the place of science in Chinese civilisation.[41]

Following the unification of China in 1949, there was a new confidence in Beijing. When the Academy of Science was founded under the presidency of a poet, historian and ideologue, all knowledge was included under Science. Many writings in China began to speak of three or four thousand years of "China's glorious scientific and cultural achievements". What made this interesting was that, for most of the hundred years before 1949, Chinese scholars had thought the opposite. No one had claimed that the Chinese people had developed science, only that Chinese civilisation had declined drastically because it had none. What China needed urgently, they thought, was scientific education. With the victory of Marxist ideologues in 1949, those who subscribed to the view that all knowledge was scientific deemed the problem to have been solved. Needham's achievements

have to be seen in this context. Although he was not the
first to study early artifacts and documents in search of
Chinese science, he was the first to take a comprehensive
view. He had stimulated new ideas about the nature of
Chinese civilisation and forced people to ask questions
that no one had cared to ask before.

In this context, one may ask, will Chinese civilisation end up as one of the many national cultural
manifestations of a single global civilisation? Will there
be something like a science civilisation with Chinese
characteristics? Can the essence of China's ancient civilisation survive, still as Chinese civilisation, but now
strongly bolstered by *keji* (the favourite phrase meaning
science and technology)? It is no accident that there has
been renewed interest in China in the idea of "Chinese
learning as foundation and Western learning for application". This again puts the emphasis on science as a
method, an instrument, and the means to master the
secrets of advanced technology in order to gain national
wealth and power.

Needham was himself clear that modern "mathemati-
cised natural science" demands a total commitment to a
philosophical position about the nature of the universe.
His efforts to find this science in Chinese civilisation
were largely to suggest that China, despite its distance
from the most recent scientific discoveries, was always
part of world history. The progress of premodern science in China might have been obstructed by political
institutions and local cultural values, but the capacity for
science was clear in what the Chinese have been able to
produce over the centuries. If a science civilisation for
China is a legitimate claim, then that would be something all Chinese can identify with and be proud of.

In the context of Anglo-Chinese encounters, is conversion to science a lucky escape for the Chinese from conversion to Christianity? It depends on how science was understood. There were at least three main approaches, the first being the most accessible and popular among the Chinese of the twentieth century. This stemmed from the view that *keji*, science as hard knowledge supportive of technology, forms the foundation of a modern country's wealth and power. This view became the core of a new Chinese secularism. The second approach was more likely to prevail among scholars and intellectuals. For many of them, science was seen primarily as a magnificent methodology for study, as a sharp instrument that brought clarity and curiosity. But there was also a third dimension, found more in the West than in China. Here science became a source of faith that led its believers to marvel at God's work on earth. There have been Europeans and Americans whose faith in Christianity was either unaffected by their study of science or was strengthened by it. Such believers are also found among the Chinese overseas, particularly among the local-born of second and third generation settlers, but few scientists on Mainland China are known to have turned to organised religion. Nevertheless, if people feel that economic success and rapid social change did little to meet their spiritual needs, the worship of science may produce new faiths. Once science no longer stands in the way of personal faith, new impulses for conversion could emerge. That faith may not be chalked up as Christian missionary success, but who can say that a conversion to science may not seed conversions of other kinds?

No conversion is ever ideal or wholly positive if taken to excess. It is ironic that science could be incompletely learned and the excesses of "scientific" socialism led Mao Zedong, with his Great Proletarian Cultural Revolution, back to the horrors of an obscurantist secular worship of a sage-leader. No Christian conversion should mean a return to superstition (*mixin*). Certainly, a blind faith in science is no protection against a blind faith in wealth and political power. The road to that power takes me to my next chapter. This is one that focuses on the fourth on Arthur Waley's list, "to rule".

5 *"To rule"*

In the last chapter, I noted that the Chinese elites were invited to consider a Christian idea of Heaven and the spiritual life it promised, but they were attracted instead to the science that would explain the mysteries in Nature and teach them how to master the resources of Earth. In the Chinese scheme of things, a separation of the three concepts of Heaven, Earth and Man was clearly recognised. This was in contrast to the dualities more familiar in the West, for example, between darkness and light, between body and soul, between what was God's and what was Caesar's. The Chinese realms of Heaven, Earth and Man reflected the three stages of life that the elites were trained to face and these found expression through the teachings of Buddhism, Taoism and Confucianism. In that context, Christianity at its most spiritual competed with Buddhist metaphysics but most Chinese thought that Christian doctrines did not offer them anything as rational, and some found Christian practices hard to distinguish from features of popular Buddhism, which Christians described as superstition. Science, on the other hand, enriched areas of knowledge on Earth that the Chinese did not have. The ends and means of this science are distinctively secular but, for the Chinese who had no experience of the tensions created by the

separation of Church and State, this was not a problem. Their Confucian elites, in particular, were educated
to emphasise this world and offered no promises about
the next. Thus, while they retained their own images
of Heaven, they and those they taught and trained for
public service willingly received what illuminated their
Earth.

"To rule", the subject of this chapter, challenged the
Chinese at the third level, the realm of Man. The core
of this realm was the way humans were organised and
governed. At its heart was the nature of power, how it
translated into authority and legitimacy, how it was used
or abused. Given the underpinnings of a strong system
of governance for over 2,000 years, Chinese elites were
not convinced that the militarily powerful British could
offer them a system of governance superior to what they
had inherited. The social and political norms that they
favoured had largely survived the initial impact of defeat by the British in the nineteenth century. The life
of Confucian service to the emperor-state, at least in
theory, remained one of secular learning. This emphasis
on learning began from childhood and was to last a lifetime. There were obvious limitations to such a heritage
and many kept themselves sane and healthy by mastering
Taoist bodily practices. When the time came for them
to leave public service, the weary functionaries prepared
themselves for the next life, turned to the Buddhist
sutras, some composing themselves not so much for
nirvana as for a Chinese ancestorhood.[1]

In today's terms, in answer to the stresses of manag-
ing industrialisation and urban living in a China rapidly
transforming itself, some Chinese seem to be seeking
the meaning of Man's place between Heaven and Earth.

After decades of debunking all religions as superstition, the Communist Party has come to realise how strong and pervasive people's spiritual needs are. They now recognise the legitimacy of established religions and customary practices among Han Chinese and certain minority groups. Those officially registered include Buddhism, Taoism, Christianity and Islam. As in the imperial past, the present leaders have confined religious practice to private worship within approved faiths that clearly accept secular authority and could not serve as sources of political rebellion. Some Chinese are unwilling to be so restricted, and they have turned to various cults and unorthodox religions, including the newly invented practices of Falungong, a new brew of ideas drawn from Buddhism, Taoism and general science. The state has asserted that this falls within the realm of Man where the right to rule is central, and the government in Beijing has so far refused to allow these practices to be legitimised.[2]

For Chinese elites over the centuries, it was in this realm of Man that their Confucian upbringing had prepared them to rule, that is, for dutiful service and political life. After 1911, given a largely incomprehensible republican framework that was described as one that would serve the interests of the majority, a fierce contest arose about how the new elites should actually rule. Where ideals and models from the outside world were concerned, they were faced with many choices. They could prepare themselves to rule China in the way countries in the West were ruled. They could sift through the many constitutional and political forms offered by the Great Powers and decide which to follow. By the end of the First World War, the British system of rule was perceived as reliable but conservative, the French and American

models as more progressive and, after the Bolshevik revolution, especially in the eyes of the young, the Soviet
Russian experiments as the most radical. They could also
pick and choose among the several models, borrowing
only those bits which could be fitted into their own traditions of governance, that is, taking only enough of each
to help them shape a new modern state. Underlying the
explorations of all these alternatives, with fierce debates
among a new generation of intellectuals and students,
was an anxious impatience to find formulas that would,
as quickly as possible, restore China to the position of
respect it had always had and bring back to it wealth and
power.

Arthur Waley's four words captured the British mix
of offerings to the Chinese rather accurately. Three out
of the four, to fight, to trade and to rule, were worldly
in ways that both the British and the Chinese could
understand. Only one, "to convert", was an important
part of the British psyche but not for the Chinese. It had
to be given its rightful place by British officials, merchants and sailors who were pious about their religion,
but it was never seen as equal with the other three, certainly not as equal as "Christians and spices" were for the
Portuguese adventurers during an earlier era. Religion
was quietly subordinated to the secular needs of empire.
And, even this British vision of Heaven was translated
by the Chinese into a secular response, a conversion to
the science of Earth. As for the secular areas, how to rule
was the central question for the educated elites.

To deal with this issue, I ask the following questions:
What did the British have to offer the Chinese? What
kinds of British rule did the Chinese actually experience?

And, what did the Chinese learn? For each of the questions, I shall also consider some of the alternatives available to the Chinese so that we might see where and why the British way prevailed in some cases and not in others.

Unlike with trade or with fighting, and unlike the conversion to science, what the British had to offer the Chinese where ruling was concerned was always indirect or peripheral. What was indirect was the knowledge gathered about the British system of government in the prime, if not unique, example of a nation-state that became the world's largest empire. Chinese mandarins had heard distantly of what the British were doing in India by the end of the eighteenth century.[3] During the next few decades, news had filtered through to them from the first Chinese to experience British administration in Penang, Malacca and Singapore, and the record there was positive. Then, with the opening of China, both in Hong Kong and the Treaty Ports, more Chinese came in contact with British officials operating through their laws and institutions. But these experiences, like those of the Chinese sojourners in British colonies in Malaya, would have to be described as peripheral in several senses of the word. They were irrelevant to the workings of the mandarinate at the Qing imperial court where real power still lay. They were only marginally important for the duties and careers of the Chinese provincial and local officials who had to deal with the British functionaries from time to time. Even for those Chinese people who chose to live under their informal or partial jurisdiction, direct contact with British systems of law and administration were rare. Only some entrepreneurial Chinese and a few specially assigned officials could be said to be regularly in touch with the machinery of British-type government on the China coast.

Nevertheless, the British did offer distinct principles of a kind of governance, notably in Shanghai, the fastest growing of the Treaty Ports.[4] But the institutions there were unique, largely an amalgam of practical methods of urban management under an evolving oligarchic structure of British businessmen assisted by some Americans in the International Settlement (later joined by one or two Japanese). The French in their settlement next door offered alternative programs of development in their sectors of control and provided interesting comparisons. Neither offered new ideas about modern governance that the Chinese could adapt for the use of the empire-state, certainly not for the mandarins who were still confident of the soundness of their own political system, at least before 1911. After the fall of the Qing dynasty, younger activists did learn about aspects of accountability and power sharing that were not found in the Chinese tradition. This awareness crept into the critiques that they devised to challenge the incompetent republican governments in Beijing during the 1912–1928 period. Enriched with more radical republican ideals taken from the French, American and Soviet Russian revolutions, new slogans were then used by various dissident groups to harass the Nanjing government of the Guomindang party that succeeded the warlords in 1928–1949.

The appointment of Robert Hart in 1863 to head the Imperial Maritime Customs at Shanghai and then as its Inspector-General in Beijing might have provided examples of relative honesty and efficiency that impressed court and provincial officials alike.[5] The fact that he remained in charge of the Customs Service for over forty years and enabled the revenues collected to help finance modern arsenals, industries and translation bureaus not only shows how he was trusted but also what impact the service had on certain areas of late Qing government. Again, no larger principles of how to rule were transmitted to the Chinese elites, only a general agreement that, beyond obvious naval and technological skills and in areas like urban order and financial control, the British did have something modern and valuable for the Chinese to learn. There was certainly no thought of replacing the ramshackle remains of the Qing bureaucracy with the modernising structures operating in Britain. What was at stake was the totality of the political system, the ideas and institutions that would underpin a new centralised government for republican China. Unlike the Japanese leaders, who could reform an administration under an emperor system that was intact, the Chinese thought that they had to start afresh. Thus the republican model remained mystifying for another decade.

For almost fifty years until the 1920s, the idea of a constitutional monarchy with a representative parliament largely consisting of two major political parties chosen by the people was still intriguing to a whole range of reformers. Knowledge of British political practices had begun to reach China through the reports, not always favourable, of ambassadors to Britain like Guo Songdao (1818–1891), Zeng Jize (1839–1890) and Xue Fucheng (1838–1894). They were at times concurrently ministers to France, Belgium and Italy and provided comments on various European systems of government that contributed to Chinese understanding of the institutions of Victorian England.[6] This was not always appreciated at a time when there was a growing reaction

by conservative mandarin critics of the seemingly pro-
Western reforms advocated by those who were members of the so-called Self-Strengthening Movement. For
them, their sacred duty was still to try and reinvigorate
traditional principles of government.

At another level, among the officials and literati outside the court, there was greater interest in the translations of books on British and European history. Such
books were read in the 1880s and 1890s by, for example, young scholars like K'ang Youwei (1858–1927)
and his contemporaries. These men sought to reform
the Qing empire by comparing the British model with
those of Japan under Meiji, Russia under Peter the Great,
and Prussia under Bismarck. The even younger Liang
Qichao stimulated a group of thinkers and politicians
to study the British way through his popular essays, and
many of them were persuaded that something like re-
sponsible and democratic government would be good
for China.[7] As for Yan Fu, the former naval student who
had studied contemporary British social thought more
successfully than the secrets of British maritime power
when he was in England, he introduced a representative selection of British ideas that influenced a whole
generation of young Chinese. Although Yan Fu might
not have presented all the nuances of such a richness of
ideas, his qualified admiration of the wealth and power-
creating capabilities of the British system of government
drew the approval of all those who read him.[8] What,
then, prevented the Chinese elites and their followers
from going further and adopting some of the ideals and
methods of British rule?

I do not think that the Chinese rejected the British
model because of the bitter memories of the Opium

War and the imperial record of British dominance and interference in Chinese affairs. The more likely reason is that the new nationalism propagated by Sun Yat-sen and his ardent followers did not allow the rebels and revolutionaries to accept a constitutional monarchy headed by a Manchu emperor and dominated by Manchu aristocrats. The Confucian commitment of loyalty to the system had been seriously diluted with the decline of the Qing empire. The idea of nation, or race, had become appealing, not least because many more Chinese were impressed by the national success of a country like Britain. Only the staunchest and most orthodox Confucians could have contemplated a monarchy that was not headed by a Han Chinese dynasty, and there were no obvious Han pretenders to the Chinese throne. The Manchus would not be acceptable because they were still regarded by many as a symbol of alien conquest that patriotic Chinese had to abjure.

Thus the nationalists rejected the monarchy and took the first step away from the British model to seek inspiration in the French and American republics. The emphasis shifted from merely reforming and strengthening the imperial system to replacing it altogether with a republican road to some kind of populist democracy. No one had any idea how this could be achieved in China. It certainly could not be done without violence. In any case, a violent overthrow of a decadent regime was very much in keeping with the heritage of political China. Once the cause of republican revolution was adopted, it was concluded that violence was unavoidable, as with the French and American revolutions. The British, with their monarchical system and a commitment to law and order as the foundations of profitable trade, could not be expected to approve of this or to help. Nor, of course, could the Japanese with their Meiji emperor system, nor the Germans with their Kaiser before 1918. When, after only two years in office, President Yuan Shikai asked his advisers in 1914 how to establish a stable government, it was ironic that an American political science professor should suggest that the president return to a monarchical system. Yuan Shikai took that advice and announced that he would proclaim himself emperor of China. He was totally surprised by the vehemence with which most educated Chinese rejected that course of action. It is uncertain whether this was mainly because of the unsavoury reputation of Yuan Shikai himself, or due to the fierce rivalries between various groups of warlords and revolutionaries. The rejection could have been a symptom of a Chinese act of "conversion" that made them ready to leap into the unknown. The dramatic and decisive act of choice could also have been a combination of all three of the reasons above.[9] But, whatever the reason, it was clear that there was no turning back to a reformed or reconstituted monarchy.

The new republic then looked for models in the United States and France. But with France equally implicated with Britain as imperialists in China, the Americans seemed to offer an acceptable modern alternative as an improved version of the traditional British model. The United States was also an example of a new nation-state, one that was perceived as already doing better than Britain and France. Furthermore, it was gaining in wealth and power without practising old-style imperialism at China's expense. Most of all, as a democratic republic free from the European entanglements that enfeebled both Britain and France during the First World

War, the American model became for some Chinese
leaders a better model for the future. It appealed specially to those who were impatient to find a new formula for power, those who wanted a quicker way to
national greatness than was represented by Britain of the
early twentieth century. No one could have predicted
then that, when the Bolshevik revolution burst upon
the scene, it would quickly become, for the majority
of the young patriots of the day, the main rival to an
Anglo-American solution for China.

Rather like the navy the Chinese had failed to build,
British ideals of government did not take during the
half-century that marked the peak of Victorian imperial
power. These ideals were quickly overtaken by events.
By the 1920s, they were overwhelmed by the growing literature of anti-imperialism drawn from Marx and
Lenin that was all the more potent when intermin-
gled with the outpourings of nationalism against foreign
dominance. As a result, other political alternatives were
steadily drowned out, including the modified British
heritage represented by the United States. The swift
success of Soviet power was greatly appealing to impatient and radicalised youth that had found the warlords,
the constitutionalists and the older nationalists ineffectual and corrupt. The appeal was, on the one hand,
dominated more by emotion and utopianism than sub-
stance and, on the other, highlighted by the promise
to a small band of dedicated revolutionaries of a more
efficient way to gain popular power.[10]

Unlike the older elites in their approach to British,
French and American political ideals, and reflecting the
visceral response to nationalism and xenophobia among
the populace, the young revolutionaries made no critical

examination of what the Marxist doctrines had to offer to preindustrial agrarian China. Indeed, little attention was paid to whether their principles could be adapted to Chinese political culture. Where was the class struggle? Where was the feudalism that had led to capitalism and the industrial revolution in Britain? Hasty attempts were made to fit Chinese history into the five stages of economic and systemic transition, failing which ready explanations were found in Marx's "Asiatic Mode of Production".[11] A nihilist urge to destroy, comparable to a sudden Zen-like enlightenment or a road-to-Damascus act of conversion, was supported by the opportunity to establish a new basis of power.

The turning away from both liberal democratic ways and their intellectual content was best captured by the discomfort the Chinese felt with the visit of Bertrand Russell in 1920. His young audience expected the most modern wisdom from this great philosopher of mathematics, science and society. They were, therefore, puzzled and disappointed when he seemed not to understand why they were so excited by a mix of nationalism, socialism and communism. He embodied a moderate British progressivism and was unsympathetic with Soviet power and the kinds of social experiments introduced in Russia.[12] In comparison, the Chinese made much more of the relatively successful tour of the American philosopher of education, John Dewey (1859–1952), who visited China soon after Russell. My father recalled his experience of the enlightenment that Dewey had brought to his generation of students when Dewey addressed them at the Nanjing Higher Normal College at the Dongnan (Southeastern) University. He and his contemporaries were taught by Dewey's Chinese students and were convinced that a new philosophical approach was needed for freeing the Chinese mind prior to rebuilding a new system of governance. For example, traditional methods of teaching should be replaced by methods that systematically opened young minds to modern ideas.[13] Although my father was to become an admirer of elitist British administration, he never lost his respect for the values that Dewey thought were fundamental to a constructive and transformative future for China.

In any case, perhaps the renowned and aristocratic Russell was not the best ambassador for British ideas. Dewey, although older, was much less famous, but his students who had invited him to China were heads of the university departments where he gave most of his lectures. He was thus better attuned to the mood of the ardent young Chinese who came to hear him. All the same, Dewey's gradualist political views had little impact beyond the schools in which his students taught, and he was no more successful than Russell in diverting the fervent young from their revolutionary paths. By the time Russell left China, the Englishman who left the strongest impression of British values was someone who had much less claim to wisdom. He was Charles Dickens (1812–1870), whose fictional portrayal of the consequences of the industrial revolution on Victorian England moved many Chinese to tears. Whenever he was quoted in that context, young Chinese saw him as having put flesh on to the cry against William Blake's "dark Satanic mills".[14]

The intense and growing rivalry between Anglo ideals on the one hand, and an internationalist anti-imperialism on the other, predated the Cold War rhetoric that the world lived with for more than four

decades after the Second World War. In China, through
the 1920s to 1940s, there was never a fair contest between the two sets of ideas. The rivalry was also complicated and distracted by a late imperialism led by Japan
that took advantage of Britain's problems in Europe with
an emergent German national socialist empire. The ex-
treme confusion as to how the modern world should be
ruled was further aggravated in China by the Japanese
invasion and, after that, a vicious civil war between militarist nationalism and peasant communism. There was,
therefore, no longer any question of what the Chinese
might have chosen from the alternative systems of governance available to them. The issue, as it has always been
throughout thousands of years of Chinese history, was a
matter of who won on the battlefield and in whose hands
that power would rest. And, as the Chinese have understood in their realm of Man, ideals – whether moral
or political – were always shaped by the victors. In their
eyes, the possibility of British ideas of how to rule was no
exception. British, or for that matter Anglo-American,
rule would have been a credible model only when it
could prove its efficacy in helping new leaders win political power. In 1949, the Chinese knew who and what
had won in China. Since the collapse of the Soviet
Union in 1991, however, they are less sure. Should they
in time come to believe that Anglo-American principles
of governance have really won out, some of them may
well consider having them revalued afresh.

　　This brings me to my second question: What sort
of British rule did the Chinese actually experience?
The right to rule after acquiring power by military victory was also confirmed by the experience of all those
Chinese who actually lived under British rule. This right

always came after the British had captured territory and put their governing system in place. Although these Chinese, as well as those living in Treaty Ports, did have direct experience of British rule, they were such a small percentage of the Chinese population that their experience must be described as peripheral. I mentioned earlier that the first Chinese who lived under some kind of British rule were those who flocked to Francis Light's Penang after 1788. They were the people in Penang whom George Leith described in 1805 as most useful for British trading interests in the region.[15] This was of course not a British discovery. The Portuguese and the Spanish had thought of the Chinese in the same way, when they found Chinese traders already active in East and Southeast Asia when they arrived in the sixteenth century. Soon afterwards, the Dutch in Batavia were similarly appreciative and skillfully used Chinese intermediaries to build up their empire in the East Indies. The English East India Company had known of these local trading networks for more than a century before the foundation of Penang. But their attention was focused on India and the Chinese were not important for them until they were ready to expand their trade to China. That very act of expansion brought them their first sizable number of Chinese "subjects".

We do not have any direct record of what these Chinese living on the periphery thought of British rule at this early phase. That they voted with their feet, especially from Malacca, various Sumatran ports, and other ports on the West Coast of the Malay Peninsula to British-ruled territories, suggests that they found the British welcoming. This was even more true of Singapore after its foundation in 1819. The speed at which

Chinese from the surrounding areas moved to the free trade and entrepot facilities that Singapore offered was astonishing. We have ample evidence to show that most Chinese traders found British rule congenial for the next 150 years.[16] In addition, Singapore became a major transit point for all Chinese going on to the Malay Peninsula, to all the major centres of development in the south, central and western parts of the Netherlands East Indies, and even further beyond to Indian Ocean ports. Thus the numbers of Chinese on the peripheries who knew something about British rule grew throughout the nineteenth century and the first half of the twentieth. But these were not people who could influence ideas and institutions in China itself.

It was not until the late nineteenth century that we begin to find Chinese comments on actual British administrative practices. By that time, the Chinese in Hong Kong and the Treaty Ports were familiar with how the British ran their affairs. There appeared a variety of sources for their comments. We have official mandarin reports on how the foreigners ran the concession areas, especially the unusual dominance of British merchants in the administration of Shanghai. These reports included the way the Chinese who were British subjects from the Straits Settlements exercised their acquired "British" rights on Chinese territory, notably places like Xiamen (Amoy) and Shantou (Swatow). There were also private notes on how, and how not, to deal with the British. The most vocal comments were found in Chinese newspapers, the earliest appearing late in the nineteenth century in Hong Kong, followed by those in Shanghai and then, at the turn of the century, also those in Singapore and Penang.[17]

It is interesting to note that the Chinese in the Straits Settlements who were the first to know the British as administrators were local-born Chinese, called "Babas" or "Straits Chinese", who recorded their favourable comments in the English language. Later, their writings in *The Straits Chinese Magazine* (1897–1907) and the finest work of history written by a Baba Chinese, Song Ong Siang's *One Hundred Years of the Chinese in Singapore*, captured the range of feelings they had for British rule. They were followed by writings in the press and speeches in the legislature that varied from gratitude for its benefits to increasing frustration at British unwillingness to let more of them partake in the tasks of governance.[18] As these writings were not available to those who did not know English and could read only Chinese, we do not know what China-born Chinese thought of them. But we can usefully compare the works in English with what was published in contemporary Chinese newspapers and appreciate the differences in outlook. In English, the stress was on respect for British law and order and, in Chinese, there was considerable appreciation of the relative freedom to trade and the autonomy to organise themselves socially.

Significantly, because the Chinese in Hong Kong wrote in Chinese from the start, it is there that the first accounts of direct Chinese experiences of the advantages of British rule are to be found. For example, we have a specific example of what politically minded Chinese thought of the government of Hong Kong in the writings of Hong Rengan (1822–1864), the cousin of Hong Xiuquan, the Taiping Heavenly Kingdom's only emperor. Too late to be of much use to his cousin, Hong Rengan's many ideas about law, banking and insurance,

roads and transportation, and matters of practical administration, as well as his views against slavery and infanti-
cide, had been stimulated by his stay in Hong Kong.[19]
Many prominent Chinese had detailed knowledge of the
practical ways the British had found to solve problems
of modern urban living in an alien land, ways which
the British were prepared to share selectively with some
of their Chinese subjects. These included some of the
compradores who worked for the larger British companies as well as the earliest Chinese members appointed
to the Legislative Council. The more articulate among
them wrote regularly for the Chinese newspapers, and
men like Hu Liyuan (1847–1916) (together with someone like Ho Kai who knew the British well) and Zheng
Guanying (1842–1921) drew on their knowledge of
British rule in some of the articles collected in their
books like *Xinzheng zhenquan* (The True Meaning of
New Governance) and *Shengshi weiyan* (Warnings to a
Prosperous Age).[20]

In particular, British ideas of medicine, hygiene and
public health attracted attention and young Chinese
were quick to look to the medical profession, as in
the example of Ho Kai himself, and the first Queen's
Scholar of Singapore, Lim Boon Keng (Lin Wenqing).
It is not surprising that the first tertiary institutions in
both Hong Kong and Singapore were medical colleges.
Less obviously, the Chinese were impressed by the uses of
common law. Mysterious though the legal system has remained for most Chinese down to the present day, many
recognised very early that it was far more equitable and
justly administered than anything that the Chinese themselves had devised. Someone like Ho Kai was moved to
take a law degree as well as his earlier medical one. His

brother-in-law, Ng Choy (Wu Tingfang, 1842–1922),
with his background in British colonies, was able to use
the legal knowledge from his training in London to become a senior official and diplomat in both imperial and
republican China.[21] Later, others from Hong Kong and
China who trained as law students in Britain also served
China as jurists and diplomats well into the 1940s. Although their numbers were small when compared with
those who studied in the United States, these suggest
that the appreciation of British rule in the medical and
legal areas was widespread and pervaded the practical
handbooks of government produced during the decades
of the Republic of China.

Less noticed at the time was the British work on harbours and roads. For those who understood this, British
contributions in these areas were truly impressive. Although literati Chinese were not attracted nor encouraged to get into engineering professions, it is striking
that the first British colonial university established east
of India, the University of Hong Kong (HKU) in 1911,
started with a Faculty of Engineering. Various Chinese provincial governments sent scholarship students
to Hong Kong to study civil engineering and return to
work in China. The best known of a very distinguished
group of engineers, Liu Xianzhou (1890–1975), ended
his career in the 1950s as vice-president of what had
become the best engineering university in China, the
famous Tsing Hua University in Beijing. The surviv-
ing HKU alumni in various parts of China down to the
present are mostly engineers and most of them remember the university and their British teachers fondly.[22]

In short, British direct rule in Hong Kong at the end
of the nineteenth and the first half of the twentieth served

as a positive example of good management of urban and mercantile affairs, notably public health, roads and the rule of law. The impact could be found even in the political doctrines of someone like Sun Yat-sen, who eventually turned away from what he saw as a conservative British model to a revolutionary Soviet type of political party-state. In his lecture at HKU in 1923, he specifically mentioned his debt to what he learnt from British rule in Hong Kong. Indeed, although less directly, many of his speeches throughout his political career, as well as his outlines and plans for China's development programs, displayed his admiration for what he saw in Britain. It was not always clear how Sun Yat-sen and his followers would have translated all that for the development of agrarian China, but in the plans for railways, mines and hydraulic projects can be found many ideas which derived directly or indirectly from Sun Yat-sen's travels around the British Empire.[23]

Herein lies an apparent difficulty in assessing the impact of British rule for the Chinese. There seemed to be a contradiction between Chinese merchants and politically conscious patriots. The merchants who experienced direct British rule learnt to respect conditions that they had not enjoyed under anyone else, notably some of the laws protecting property, patents and contracts and the relative fairness in administrative decisions. The patriots who could be found in all classes, however, identified much that the British had done, and were doing, in China and elsewhere with colonial exploitation. This was true even when, as on the Chinese mainland, the British had never exercised colonial rule but were primarily symbols of imperialism. For the merchant class, the British taught them that stability, legal predictability and relative freedom were desirable no matter who the rulers were. For the patriots, national sovereignty, cultural respect and ethnic identity were uppermost and there could be no compromise with alien rule.

But the contradiction is more apparent than real if we look at the last decades of two examples of British rule in eastern Asia: that in Malaya (now West Malaysia and Singapore) and Hong Kong. I shall not go into the complex triangular relations of the British, the Malays and the Chinese in the Malay States, but focus only on how British rule appeared to the divided Chinese communities and how the British managed the various divisions. The Chinese were initially divided by their native-place origins and by the mutually incomprehensible dialects they spoke. They formed clan and district associations that drew together members of the same dialect or surname group. The British saw these associations as contributing on the whole to social stability and tolerated and supervised their exclusive organisations. With the advent of Chinese nationalism, there were new divisions among the Chinese, between those who responded to politics imported from China and those who emphasised a local loyalty, especially between those who went to Chinese schools and learnt a common Mandarin language and those who studied in English-medium schools. Here the British clearly favoured the latter and did not hesitate to deport anyone not born in their colonies and protectorates who went beyond the defined limits to their political activities.[24]

Then came newer divisions among the nationalists themselves, between those who supported the Nationalist regime and those who were won over by Mao Zedong's Communist Party. The British constrained the

activities of both groups carefully but then recruited
some of them, including communists and left-wing nationalists, to fight the common Japanese enemy during
the Second World War.[25] The most notable contributions came from those who joined British forces
against the occupation of Malaya in 1942–1945. The
best known of them, Lim Bo Seng (Lin Mousheng,
1909–1944), studied in Singapore and then at the University of Hong Kong. He then joined "Force 136",
the Anglo-Chinese military unit that sent him back
to Malaya, where he was caught and executed by the
Japanese. Thereafter, the Malayan Communist Party,
which claimed to be nationalist as well as anti-imperialist
but was largely led by Chinese cadres, turned itself into
a local party seeking independence for Malaya.

To deal with this threat in the post-war anti-colonial
atmosphere, the British encouraged both an ideological
divide among the Chinese and a racial divide between
the Malays and the Chinese. Thus the various Chinese
communities faced a new reality in which they had to
choose between two courses. They could fight for a local
communist victory as in China, or support the British
plan for a multiracial society in which loyal Chinese
would be accepted as citizens in an eventual Malayan
state. In that context, the majority of Chinese voted for
the law and order, racial harmony, relative freedom and
the ethnic autonomy that the British promised. There
was much talk about British cunning in looking after
their own long-term interest in independent Malaya, but
surprisingly little doubt among most local Chinese that
the British could, and would, deliver on their promises.[26]

In the case of Singapore, three-quarters of the population of this British colony was of Chinese descent by the

second half of the nineteenth century, and this remains so after over forty years of self-rule and independence. Although it was never intended that there would be an independent republic of Singapore, that Chinese element in the population has become the beneficiaries of the British administrative and legal heritage left to them after its separation from Malaysia in 1965. Their leaders after independence have fought off the challenge of British-type democratic politics in favour of the bureaucratic status quo of the multiracial commercial metropolis that the British left behind. How this was done has been succinctly described in Lee Kuan Yew's memoirs.[27] He has made it clear that he saw no contradiction between the needs of an international market economy and the nation-building that he set out to shape. Having a largely Chinese electorate, he devised a party system to ensure that a clear majority would be satisfied with an honest and efficient bureaucracy, one that conformed to a post-Confucian ideal that he believes British democracy could not have provided. The governing People's Action Party has calculated that, for most Chinese, the weighting given to economic over political freedoms was something they could live with. How well this amalgam of two different ideals will survive is yet unknown. The experiment reminds us, however, that Chinese who have lived under the British have found ways not only to adapt themselves to British rule but also, when appropriate or necessary, to appropriate some of the methods of governance for their particular needs.

The Hong Kong story is more complicated but even more illuminating. British rule there since the end of the Second World War, and particularly since the process of global decolonisation of the 1950s, had been changing over several decades to fit the environment of revolutionary China.[28] The Chinese who experienced that rule from 1949 to 1984 could not but have noted how adaptable the British were in the face of continuous uncertainty. The post-war generation of local British colonial officials endured and survived many kinds of threat to the colony's stability. Hong Kong's population more than trebled during that period because of the unending flood of immigrants from the mainland. Throughout that time, there were passionate supporters of both the People's Republic of China and the Republic of China in Taiwan plotting to outdo each other in gaining influence over the Hong Kong government. In addition, there was a growing number of Hong Kongers who wanted either a British status quo or some kind of independence. Their comments about what they thought of British rule, increasingly expressed in one of the freest presses in the world, ranged from tolerance to resigned acceptance and even open admiration.

The civil service was steadily localised as more and more Hong Kong Chinese were recruited and trained to take over when their British seniors retired and to run Hong Kong after they all left. All of them, whether of British or Hong Kong origins, struggled to be humane and responsive, draconian and legalistic, diplomatic and evasive, reasonably honest and efficient, all at the same time and not always successfully. They were sensitive to the fact that they were serving on the frontline of the Cold War in Asia, and were mostly providing support to one side against the other. Despite the exhortations to be alert and grasp the opportunities to be knowledgeable about developments in the PRC, they were often taken

by surprise. In particular, they had to scramble to cope
when millions across the border faced starvation in the
early 1960s and when the Cultural Revolution turned
murderous and spilled over into the territory at the end
of the sixties. Understandably, they could not meet all the
needs of the political refugees who were allowed to stay.
But they did provide something that was nothing short
of miraculous. They sustained faith among the colony's
Chinese population in a system of modern urban government that kept trade open and freedom sacrosanct. It
is a paradox that while there was no democracy in Hong
Kong, and it has only a very limited democracy today, it
remains one of the freest societies in Asia.[29]

After weathering the storms from Mao Zedong's
China for thirty years, Hong Kong reaped the rich har-
vest of Deng Xiaoping's economic reforms. For two
years between 1982 and 1984, all was uncertain while
British and Chinese officials debated the terms of the
return of Hong Kong to China. Once again, the governing system stood up to the strain and prepared carefully for the uncharted autonomy that had been devised
for Hong Kong through a newly invented Basic Law.
Although there remains skepticism about the long-term
impact of that Law on the fate of Hong Kong within
the PRC, the negotiations between Hong Kong and
PRC representatives were conducted broadly along lines
determined in the Sino-British Declaration of 1984.
In short, the Hong Kong representatives kept their
eyes firmly on the British-inspired institutions that they
wanted to preserve and the PRC representatives were
prepared to accommodate as many of these as they could.
Underlying the extended discussions on both sides were

pragmatic attitudes that set out to ensure that an administrative structure that would support a stable trading and financial environment would be retained.

From 1984 until the actual handover in 1997, we have a much more self-conscious record of how British rule appeared to a variety of Chinese both inside and outside China. The details of that story still need to be told, but we know enough to conclude that the system of executive-led government that evolved under British management in Hong Kong has evoked admiration on the mainland. The framework that had been refined to meet the needs of a global market economy was just what the Chinese leaders needed to prepare their own reformist transitions so that China could safely open itself to the world.

I said earlier that British rule for the Chinese was either indirect or peripheral. It is surprising how either, or both, could still be influential. This brings me to my last question: What did the Chinese learn from British rule? Let me not suggest that the Chinese learnt a great deal from Britain. In my opening chapter, I made a brief comparison between Anglo-Indian encounters and Anglo-Chinese ones and said I would not try to explain why the former seemed more fruitful than the latter. Mahatma Gandhi had rejected the ideas behind the words "to convert, trade, rule and fight", whereas Chinese leaders responded to all four of them. But one obvious point from the examples of British rule I have just given needs to be mentioned. Where the Chinese have lived for long periods under British rule, as in Malaya and Hong Kong, they have not only been willing to accept that rule but even shown a readiness to emulate, or continue with, British ideals of modern government.

This was particularly obvious when it was clearly in their interest to do so. And when this happened, most British laws and institutions have survived remarkably well, including those pertaining to education, transport, health, drainage, prisons, and even emergency regulations and internal security acts, which were in the main refurbished after British departure. If the factor of time was decisive, it may help explain why the British in India have left a fuller legacy. In China, except for some peripheral areas, the British were not there for anywhere as long and were never in charge. What had begun as fighting in a most aggressive way was soon diverted into extensive and profitable trading, and the remaining energy was dispersed in trying to convert some rather intransigent Chinese.

Yet it would be premature to dismiss the indirect and peripheral influences in the larger context of an Anglo-American political heritage in the new global market economy. An early indication of this development may be found in the cooperation between Britain and the United States over Hong Kong since the 1950s. This was very discreetly managed for the first thirty years of the People's Republic of China, with China accepting the mutual benefits of a controlled but porous border at Shenzhen. The story of the non-hostile and parallel development that both sides managed during that period will make fascinating reading when it is fully told. In time, it may well be seen as the most sustained period of Anglo-Chinese understanding in the 155 years of a wary relationship, a set of encounters that engendered valuable lessons about governance on both sides of that border. What the British in Hong Kong learnt to do may never have relevance in Britain itself, but that the

politically sensitive and administratively fruitful connections of 1949–1997 laid new foundations for Hong Kong
governance cannot be denied. Once it was clear by the
1960s that Hong Kong would never be an independent country but would eventually return to Chinese
sovereignty, there was a coming together of ends and
means among all concerned. That was inevitable once
it became necessary to have a realistic timetable for the
British to leave.[30] On both sides, for some thirty years,
officials strained to learn about one another in order
to prepare for a special administration that Hong Kong
would be allowed to have one day within the People's
Republic of China. That would also enable the central
officials in Beijing to accustom themselves to what was
not immediately digestible in Hong Kong's system of
governance.

But no one could have predicted the turnaround in
the PRC following the death of Mao Zedong. The
Hong Kong issue became more urgent and open when
Deng Xiaoping decided on a series of radical economic
reforms and in 1982 took up the delicate negotiations
over Hong Kong's eventual return to China. Once
those negotiations began, the pressure on both sides to
understand the divergent principles of government that
had to be reconciled before Hong Kong's handover in
1997 became increasingly strong. The political lessons
of the 1982–1984 Sino-British meetings were followed
by equally thorough discussions about how Hong Kong
should be ruled between Chinese on both sides of
the border. In the talks between the representatives of
Beijing and those of the Hong Kong communities,
drawing up the Basic Law for the Hong Kong Special
Administrative Region involved a delving into the

relevant detailed workings of the Hong Kong and PRC governments that neither side had ever done before. It is not yet clear precisely what benefits each side had gained from such detailed debates. Certainly, each had begun with many prejudices and misunderstandings about the workings of government on the other side. But there is evidence that both sides learnt a great deal from the years of give and take. However unequal that process might have appeared to the people of Hong Kong, the final shape of the Basic Law shows that the Chinese officials have learnt something of the art of British colonial rule and administration well. They have found most of the institutions acceptable to the future Hong Kong they will have within China. The British Foreign Office, monitoring and trying to guide the Hong Kong side, seemed to have also been content that the essentials of their heritage would stay. The last-minute calls for democracy simply reflected a deeper unease that really emerged with dramatic events in China itself.

The change came in 1989, after the Tiananmen tragedy and particularly after the end of the Soviet system and the end of the Cold War when the United States and, by extension, Western Europe, no longer needed a "China card" to play against Soviet power. That meant that they stopped tolerating the illiberal policies that they had been willing to overlook when they needed to have China on side. There followed a major change of direction when China's increasingly radical economic reforms provided new opportunities to introduce Anglo-American political ideals more directly into the territory. The last years of Christopher Patten's governorship brought this to the surface for Hong Kong Chinese. They led to a high degree of discomfort for all

the Chinese involved and alerted the elites in Beijing
to a new political offensive that they saw as potentially
destabilising for them.[31] This is a story that is still un-
folding and this is not the place to speculate about its
outcome. But it is likely that British rule in Asia through
a highly dedicated professional bureaucracy, as modified
for Chinese subjects in Hong Kong, could offer useful
examples for an evolving Chinese system of government
for the future. It is interesting that British political ideals
about parliamentary democracy had never been considered on their own merits, but British governing practices have attracted respect. Chinese experiences of these
practices may still have an influence beyond expectations, especially with examples like Singapore and Hong
Kong where the influences are better appreciated after
the British themselves have left. Success on the ground
is still the best teacher for pragmatic Chinese leaders.
Indirect and peripheral it may have been, but British
rule as introduced in modernising cities seems to have
life in East Asia yet.

6 Beyond Waley's list

"For many years past Chinese students had been coming to England for technical education. Those at Cambridge came chiefly from Singapore, and many of them could not speak, still less read, Chinese." With these few words, Arthur Waley's 1942 essay dismissed the Chinese of the British Commonwealth.[1] This had been true of Ku Hung-ming and Song Ong Siang, partially true of Lim Boon Keng and Wu Lien-teh, and then only too true again of those who went to study in Britain during the 1930s. The Chinese students who came from Hong Kong were better in Chinese, but not those who came from the Dominions or the West Indies. The paradox is that many of the Chinese of that period found themselves after graduation in the service of China, where they would have to learn the Chinese language on the job.

Thus, until the 1950s, when we speak of the Chinese in the Commonwealth, we would find notable traces of their relations with China. That trend was reversed after Mao Zedong's Great Leap Forward, and even more decisively after the Cultural Revolution of 1966–1976. Then, during the years 1984–1997, preparations were made for some six million Chinese in Hong Kong to leave the Commonwealth and become part of the PRC on Mainland China. By the beginning of the twenty-first century, about thirteen million people of Chinese descent remain in the Commonwealth, four-fifths of them in Malaysia and Singapore and the rest in the former Dominions. If we include the whole of the English-speaking world, the figure would be closer to fifteen million, somewhat more than half of the Chinese outside China (the PRC, Taiwan, Hong Kong and Macau). Apart from some of the most recent immigrants, hardly any of these Chinese now look to China as home.[2]

But Waley had grasped a larger reality. "A great turning-point in our relations with China had come", he said of the 1900s and 1910s. The fact was that, when he wrote these words in 1942, an even greater turning point was on the horizon, one that was accompanied by a reassessment of the Commonwealth's place in Asia. Hong Kong had become its eastern edge, Malaysia and Singapore the key links with Australia, New Zealand and the South Pacific. The deep involvement with China, begun with the Opium War, had reached the final act. There may be appearing a new story of Anglo encounters with Chinese who have settled outside China, one that is quite separate from those with the Chinese in China. But, with the former, the story is not yet ready to be told. This is, therefore, a good time to look over the asymmetrical earlier encounters where, as Waley's four words show, it was not so much what he had called "A Debt to China", but more like the debt to Britain that many Chinese elites, whether they liked it or not, had to live with.[3]

I promised to offer a longer view of Anglo-Chinese encounters. Clearly the threat that the British had first brought from the sea has transformed China's strategic thinking. If the Chinese leaders still perceive that the threat remains, now coming from the Asia-Pacific region itself, they would have learnt some lessons from their earlier efforts to build up their naval forces. This has already had a considerable impact on the region. The British had helped greatly in modernising the ports and harbours if not the navy itself, and the Americans have given the most sophisticated training to the Chinese in Taiwan to fight at sea and in the air. This will challenge the Mainland Chinese to greater efforts to secure their maritime interests. This may well be Britain's most lasting impact on Chinese history.

But the lesson learnt goes well beyond the navy. What was all the earlier fighting about and what kind of fighting lies ahead? The Chinese have stressed again and again that, in building up their forces, they want no more than to defend their lands and their sovereignty. Drawing upon the recent histories of militarist Germany and Japan, foreign strategic thinkers have found it difficult to believe this. They fear that the century of humiliation and grievance will not allow the new Chinese leaders to stop at defence. Also, China's years of exposure to an internationalist communism would have whetted the country's appetite for a larger global role. The Chinese leaders, on their part, refuse to see any analogy between their limited concerns and German and Japanese ambitions during the first half of the twentieth century. If anything, they feel insulted by the comparisons. They point to the tradition of restraint whenever the Chinese empire was strong and to their defensive policies when China was threatened by alien conquest. They argue that their land borders remain as vulnerable as ever, even though Russia is weaker now, the Central Asian Muslim powers are disunited, and India only just beginning to be fiercely nationalistic. Also, the threat of an Anglo-American cordon allied to a potentially powerful Japan remains alive, even though the British role may now be much reduced in both Hong Kong and Taiwan.

Contemporary historians draw attention to the land wars that the PRC has been involved in since 1949 as evidence of China's readiness to fight outside its own borders against its neighbours. In particular, they refer to the Chinese role in the Korean and Vietnam wars against what were in effect alliances led by the United States. And they point to the 1962 war over the Indian borders that the British had left so ill-defined, the skirmishes with Soviet Russia in the 1960s and 1970s, and the pre-emptive attack on Vietnam in 1979. There have also been fears of China's long-term expansion plans for domination of the South China Sea on the basis of questionable historical claims extended to the Spratly Islands. Certainly the animosity in Sino-Vietnamese relations over the islands that each side controls suggests that these claims are unlikely to be resolved easily. The Chinese continue to deny any aggressive designs, asserting only their right to secure their borders, not just on land but also now at sea. The overland dangers to China's security they have always known how to handle, but the efforts to build naval forces to deal with enemies along China's coasts have caused the Chinese great difficulties and also aroused much anxiety among neighbours who have not seen a credible Chinese navy reaching out beyond China's shores for over 500 years.

The full weight of the latter experience cannot, of course, be laid at the door of the British. The French, the Russians and the Japanese all made major contributions to China's sense of insecurity before 1945, while Russian and American pressures grew more oppressive from the 1950s. It is clear that the influence of the latter two powers on Chinese strategic thinking has been great. It might even be said that these pressures have dramatically improved China's capacity to fight since then, and that the benefits for a modern military force have been incalculable. The total impact on China may be compared to the heritage of the British military tradition in India and elsewhere in the Commonwealth. That heritage has made a difference to the armed forces of both China and India, albeit in different ways. How longer-term Chinese ideas about security and defence, as well as about global strategic thinking, have changed will call for close examination for decades to come.

What the Chinese learnt from the British about methods of trading and how much it is now understood that business enterprises should be protected by law is still controversial. If the historians in China continue to believe that the first breach of China's coastal defences in the 1840s was only about unscrupulous traders selling opium, and dismiss the underlying concepts of the freedom to trade as one of the main reasons for the war, it is unlikely that trade will ever occupy the same important position in China as in the Anglo world. But there is no doubting that changes in the role of Chinese merchants have been profound. Even if Chinese governments may never protect their merchants in the same way, the recognition that entrepreneurs deserve a higher social status is now well recognised. In 2001, the Communist Party's secretary-general suggested that the Party consider admitting successful businessmen as members.[4] That some of these entrepreneurs now have a place in politics and may be entrusted with a share of power is another shift in cultural values that followed the British encounters. The Chinese both within the PRC and outside have been studying the current Anglo-American models with great care. These models have already transformed business organisations and practices among the Chinese outside, and are bound to influence the future of private enterprise on the mainland.

The ongoing debates about public versus private management of both domestic and foreign trade have gone through many twists and turns. They are likely to go on providing lessons both in merchant control and participation. What is intriguing is how the political language is adapting to economic realities. Will China move away from variants of state or welfare capitalism with Chinese characteristics so that they meet and blend with the forms of "Chinese capitalism" said to be taking shape among the Chinese overseas? What innovations are possible when a state run by a communist party adapts more thoroughly to the dictates of a global market economy? The evidence of hard-nosed pragmatism behind decision-making on the mainland is stronger than ever. While this is familiar in the larger context of Chinese history and culture, never before have Chinese leaders recognised a connection between trading success and higher standards of living for all Chinese. Nor have so many of them been so alert about the changing conditions of the world outside, not least the community leaders among the Chinese who have chosen to settle there. Does this mean that China's worldview is about to be transformed? It is probably not enough that trading practices conform to the global standards now dominated by English-speaking businessmen. A change in the Chinese cast of mind is needed and the conversion to new faiths so far is still incomplete.

The British had, from the beginning, offered Christianity accompanied by better gunboats and engineering, and the Chinese chose the latter to defend Chinese civilisation against the former. The decision led them to modern science, the force of which has shaken Chinese faith in older methods of technical innovation and ultimately in the older morality that supported their lives. Anglo modes of scientific thought have brought a genuine liberation for most Chinese. Although the impact on their spiritual life has been uneven, the systematic removal of barriers to nation-wide communication has had revolutionary consequences on the contemporary common language. The extensive use of that language in all modern schools and all sections of the media has laid new foundations for a distinctive national identity. But the traditional spirit of "Confucianist" orthodoxy and "Taoistic" dissent, if not defiance, still resists the allures of science. It provides an undertow that channels contemporary political behaviour, but this remains far from the liberal secular ideals that the British have cultivated for the past two hundred years.

The scientific conversion and the consequences for Chinese education have had a profound impact. How far this will go in transforming all aspects of Chinese thought and action is yet unclear, but there are signs that more doors to fresh rethinking about every aspect of received wisdom are being opened wide. One test of the extent of this change would be to ask whether it could translate into scientific attitudes in the social sciences in the new universities. If the universities in Taiwan and Hong Kong are anything to go by, further influences in the Chinese realm of Man are bound to occur. Recent changes in the respective academies, the Academy of Science and Academy of Social Sciences on the mainland and the Academia Sinica in Taiwan, suggest that new kinds of social science professionals will join the scientists and engineers as a respectable class before long.[5] Thus, although there was no direct impact of the Christian faith that many British missionaries had hoped for, the secular conversions have kept open the question of intellectual freedom and that may yet, however indirectly, extend the religious freedoms that the Chinese people wish to enjoy.

British rule as an experience has obviously not run its course. The Chinese leaders in the PRC have shown appreciation of the executive-led governments that the British evolved in their plural-society colonies. Those that have been successful in offering stability to multi-racial, multi-religious, multi-lingual societies and have now become nation-states, like Malaysia and Singapore, are particularly impressive. The governance of Hong Kong, however, would be the most familiar to them. It has fed their reservations about multi-party politics and encouraged them to experiment with and extend their one-party state system. Eventually, if they can stave off the pressures there for multi-party democracy, this may lead them to a kind of "no-party" state, embracing all people, that is closer to their own political traditions.[6] If that happens, it will be a system modernised to be essentially an integrated military, civil and party "mandarinate", that is, something comparable to what used to prevail in British colonies but now adapted and restructured for Chinese rule.

Beyond that, it is clear that what has underlined Chinese responses to governance during the past century is the Chinese discovery of the power of the modern sovereign nation-state. They have been forced to reassess their identity as a state, whether based on an ancient but revitalised civilisation or on borders established by a past empire. They recognise that any system that offers them maximum security both within and without after a century of humiliation would greatly help them create a modern nation. Such a system would include lessons from the British rule that many Chinese have experienced, whether directly or indirectly. Not all Chinese leaders will appreciate the full ramifications of the British principles of governance, but their encounters with practices that respect the law, and produce the framework for civic discipline and general orderliness, will not be easily forgotten.

The Chinese, including all those who have lived, and still live, in Commonwealth countries, have not and cannot now be expected to produce men like Jan Christiaan Smuts and his generation of leaders who came out of the crucible of the British Empire and devoted themselves to perpetuating the Commonwealth. That time has passed. But there have been examples in Malaysia and Singapore of leaders of Chinese descent who have appreciated the virtues of that body. And there may be others in former Dominions like Australia and Canada who are ready to do their bit to strengthen the historic ties that bind them to Britain. The greater potential, however, is to be found among those Chinese who now use English as their "mother tongue" and write their poetry, fiction, scientific and scholarly treatises in the language as well as any Englishman would. Waley was fascinated with Xu Zhimo's infatuation with things English and described the appointment in 1941 of Chen Yinke (Ch'en Yin-k'o, 1890–1969) to the Chair of Chinese at Oxford as "the most important event that has ever occurred in the history of Chinese-European relations".[7] Waley was right in that, for that time, it really would have been a new kind of encounter. Since then, in the literary and academic areas, such examples have been multiplied many times over. While not all would illuminate Anglo-Chinese encounters equally, their cumulative impact throughout the Commonwealth as well as the Anglo world of the United States is impressive. It reminds us that, when the terms of respect are right, the broader experience beyond colonies and dominions can be much more enriching.

More relevant to the specific relations between the British and the Chinese are the other words in Arthur Waley's list of 1942, which I have not dealt with in this series of lectures. Waley noted "a turning-point" when the British who visited China were not only "missionaries, soldiers, sailors, merchants or officials", but included men of leisure, poets, professors, thinkers who began to go to China simply "to make friends and learn". He may have been prescient about a new generation of sinologists and future professors who emerged after the end of the Second World War, but was still well ahead of his times. Where the men of leisure, poets and thinkers were concerned, the people he had in mind were far from typical. Certainly Lowes Dickinson was impressed by the China that Waley himself had drawn from past glories. E. M. Forster obviously had a soft spot for Xiao Qian, and was probably not aware how unusual it was for a

Chinese to appreciate modern English literature as much as he did. In addition, there were other English men and women, like Kingsley Martin (1897–1969), George Orwell (1903–1950), the leaders of the Quaker movement, who joined Bertrand Russell in urging Britain and other Western powers to prevent China from being conquered by the Japanese. It is telling that the great names of "Our Age", recorded by someone knowledgeable, and in the British cultural mainstream, like Noel Annan, do not include anyone who had much interest in China. After all, even Waley did not see fit to visit China but was content to learn from afar. This meant leaving it, with a few remarkable exceptions, mainly to officials and merchants for at least another generation.[8]

Anglo-Chinese encounters did not produce a Rudyard Kipling (1865–1936) for China, or an E. M. Forster, if we confine ourselves to Commonwealth writers. The only one who may be said to have come close was Pearl S. Buck (1892–1973), daughter of American missionaries and the first person to succeed in gaining popular concern in the West for ordinary Chinese people.[9] More recently, there have been popular British novelists whose fictional protagonists have skillfully used the Chinese stage for their exploits, but the quality of what they have written cannot compare with those writings that have been inspired by the countries of the Commonwealth itself.

The British have used China to draw their own lessons, as suggested in the stylised books by G. Lowes Dickinson (*Letters from John Chinaman*) and Ernest Bramah (1868–1942) (*Kai Lung unrolls his mat*), but these works were little known, even among the best-educated Chinese.[10] By the 1930s, Harold Acton (1904–1994) had become a new kind of literary friend for China, but he cannot adequately represent Waley's words about making friends and learning.[11] I have mentioned James Legge and Joseph Needham as one kind of friend, and one kind of learning. Arthur Waley himself would stand for another. But I cannot do justice to the topic here and will have to leave that to another day.

Waley's reference to a "turning point" during the first half of the twentieth century was probably premature. As long as the empire still seemed to be in the ascendant, there was no point turning away from the symbols of power. Where the Chinese were concerned, the endgame in Hong Kong in 1984–1997 might have been a more telling point of a terminal change. Chinese all over the world watched the last performances for signs that there might be a new beginning for Anglo-Chinese encounters when the British will mainly go to China to make friends and to learn. But the picture has not been clear. The deeper involvement of the United States as the Anglo successor since the end of the Second World War seemed to have blurred the American image among the Chinese. There had not been, before the Second World War, many American soldiers, sailors and officials, mainly traders and missionaries. Among the missionaries were many who were professors, teachers and doctors who had gone to China "to make friends", and some even "to learn". Today, professors and teachers are still going. Instead of men of leisure, there are large numbers of tourists whom the Chinese welcome. Instead of poets and thinkers, there are many more scientists, engineers and social scientists and indeed most of them make good friends. But, as long as the United States seems to have shouldered the Anglo imperial heritage, some of those who go to China may be seen as acting on behalf of the "soldiers, sailors and officials" of empire never before associated with the United States. This is, of course, not Waley's story. His profound understanding of a China long gone by had led him to a happy ending. Following an outline of 200 years of Anglo-Chinese encounters, from Penang and Singapore to the departure from Hong Kong, makes it possible to see that such an ending is still a realistic one.

Notes

1 Introduction

1 W. K. Hancock, *Smuts, Volume 1: The Sanguine Years, 1870–1919*; and *Smuts, Volume 2: The Fields of Force, 1919–1950*. Cambridge: Cambridge University Press, 1962; 1968.

2 Malaya, or British Malaya, refers to the Straits Settlements, the Federated Malay States and Unfederated Malay States before 1948, and the Federation of Malaya and the colony of Singapore until the formation of Malaysia in 1963.

3 My father was Wang Fo-wen (1903–1972). He graduated from Southeastern University, later called National Central, and now Nanjing, University. He taught in Singapore, Kuala Lumpur and Malacca before going to Surabaya. When he started working in Perak in 1932, the Great Depression had come upon Malaya and there was much labour unrest among the unemployed Chinese. Governor Cecil Clementi (1930–1934) had begun to crack down on the bitter struggle between supporters of the Nationalist Party and the Communist Party in China which he thought could only bring trouble to Malaya. The use of Chinese schools as part of that battlefield was unacceptable in multi-communal Malaya, and a school inspector's job was unavoidably politicised. As something of a "Chinese expatriate", my father kept his conscience clear by giving his first loyalty to the cause of Chinese education and teaching his only child that China was his country. He was truly a *huaqiao*, a Chinese sojourner or "Overseas Chinese". For the post-War

151

period, I use Chinese overseas. This indicates that they are no longer only temporarily away from China and focuses on the fact that they have become ethnic Chinese who have settled abroad.

The depth of his commitment to Chinese literary and artistic traditions may be seen in his collected writings, *Wang Fo-wen jinianji* (Wang Fo-wen, 1903–1972: a memorial collection of poems, essays and calligraphy). Edited by Wang Gungwu. River Edge, N.J.: Global Publishing, 2002.

4 Three of my four teachers at the University of Malaya in Singapore from 1949 to 1954 were Cambridge men: Cyril Northcote Parkinson (1909–1993), Eric T. Stokes (1924–1981) and Ian McGregor. My first teacher, Brian Harrison (1909–1995), left to take the Chair of History at the University of Hong Kong.

5 University of Malaya, Singapore (as student, 1949–54, as lecturer, 1957–59); School of Oriental and African Studies, University of London (as PhD student, 1954–1957); University of Malaya, Kuala Lumpur (1959–1968); Australian National University (1968–1986); University of Hong Kong (1986–1995); National University of Singapore (since 1997).

6 Gillian Beer, *Open Fields: Science in Cultural Encounter*. Oxford: Clarendon Press, 1996, p. 2. Her caution that encounters do not "guarantee understanding", and may only emphasise "what's incommensurate", captures my efforts here rather well.

7 I am familiar with references to a diary Ghalib had kept at the time of the Indian Mutiny and a few of the *ghazals* translated in the volume on his life and letters edited by Ralph Russell and Khurshidul Islam, *Ghalib, 1797–1869. Volume One: Life and Letters* (UNESCO Collection of Representative Works, Indian series). Cambridge, Mass.: Harvard University Press,

1969. He was a close friend of Sir Sayyid Ahmad Khan and his family.

8 Ghalib wrote this as part of a verse introduction to Sir Sayyid Ahmad Khan's edition of *Ain i Akbari*, which describes the system of administration under the great Mughal emperor Akbar (1556–1605). Ghalib was not impressed by the Mughal system and thought the edition pointless. Understandably, Sayyid Ahmad Khan did not use the introduction; Russell and Islam eds, *Ghalib*, pp. 90–91. The lines here are quoted in Rajmohan Gandhi, *Revenge and Reconciliation: Understanding South Asian History*. Delhi and London: Penguin Books India, 1999, p. 136, which quotes from Hafeez Malik, *Sir Sayyid Ahmad Kahn and Muslim Modernisation in India and Pakistan*. New York: Columbia University Press, 1980, p. 58.

9 Hsiao Ch'ien (Xiao Qian, compiler), *A Harp with a Thousand Strings: a Chinese anthology in six parts*. London: Pilot Press, 1944, pp. 381–383.

10 Ivan Morris, "The genius of Arthur Waley", in *Madly Singing in the Mountains: an Appreciation and Anthology of Arthur Waley*. Edited by Ivan Morris. London: George Allen & Unwin, 1970, p. 80.

11 Hancock, *Smuts*, vol. 2, p. 283.

12 Hancock, *Smuts*, vol. 2, p. 473.

2 "To fight"

1 Lo Jung-pang, "The emergence of China as a sea-power during the late Sung and early Yuan periods", *Far Eastern Quarterly*, 1955, vol. 14, pp. 489–503.

2 The Muslim eunuch, Admiral Zheng He, and his colleagues were sent on six major expeditions, followed by the seventh and last sent by Yongle's grandson, the Emperor Xuande (1424–1435), before the decision was made to stop these expeditions altogether. Ma Huan,

Ying-yai sheng-lan (The overall survey of the ocean's shores) [1433]. Translated from the Chinese by J. V. G. Mills. Cambridge: Cambridge University Press, for the Hakluyt Society, 1970; J. J. L. Duyvendak, "Ma Huan re-examined", *Verhandelingen d. Koninklijke Akademie v. Wetenschappen te Amsterdam*, 32, no. 3, 1933. A recent account is Louise Levathes, *When China Ruled the Seas: the treasure fleet of the Dragon Throne 1405–1433*. New York: Simon & Schuster, 1994.

For the 16th and 17th centuries, the following make interesting reading: So Kwan-wai, *Japanese Piracy in Ming China during the 16th Century*. East Lansing: Michigan State University Press, 1975; Bruce Swanson, *Eighth Voyage of the Dragon: a history of China's quest for seapower*. Annapolis, Md.: Naval Institute Press, 1982; and Ralph C. Croizier, *Koxinga and Chinese Nationalism: history, myth, and the hero*. Cambridge: East Asian Research Center, Harvard, 1977.

3 The bicentenary of the Macartney Mission aroused renewed attention for this particular moment in Anglo-Chinese relations. The approach focusing on cultural conflict was followed by Alain Peyrefitte in *The Immobile Empire* (translated from the French by Jon Rothschild). New York: Knopf and Random House, 1992. A more unconventional study offering fresh perspectives was James L. Hevia, *Cherishing Men from Afar: Qing Guest Ritual and the Macartney Embassy of 1793*. Durham, N.C.: Duke University Press, 1995.

4 Chang, Hsin-pao, *Commissioner Lin and the Opium War*. Cambridge, Mass.: Harvard University Press, 1964. A collection of documents on the hostility towards the British troops at Sanyuanli illustrates contemporary attitudes and subsequent interpretations; Guangdong sheng wenshi yanjiuguan, ed. *Sanyuanli renmin kang Ying douzheng shiliao* (Documents on the anti-British struggle

by the people of Sanyuanli). Beijing: Zhonghua Publishing, 1978.

5 Frederic Wakeman, Jr, *Strangers at the Gate: Social Disorder in South China, 1839–1861.* Berkeley: University of California Press, 1966. Philip A. Kuhn provides a larger background in "The Taiping Rebellion", in John K. Fairbank, ed. *The Cambridge History of China.* Volume 10, Part 1. Cambridge: Cambridge University Press, 1978, pp. 264–317; and *Rebellion and its Enemies in Late Imperial China, militarization and social structure, 1796–1864.* Cambridge, Mass.: Harvard University Press, 1964.

6 Liu Kwang-ching, "The Ch'ing Restoration". In Fairbank, ed. *Cambridge History*, pp. 409–434, 456–477; Andrew Wilson, *The "Ever-victorious Army": a history of the Chinese campaign under Lt.-Col. C. G. Gordon and of the Suppression of the Tai-ping Rebellion.* Edinburgh: William Blackwood, 1868; William Hail, *Tseng Kuo-fan and the Taiping Rebellion, with a short sketch of his later career.* New York: Paragon Book Reprint Corp., 1964. Second Edition.

7 Jane Kate Leonard, *Wei Yuan and China's Rediscovery of the Maritime World.* Cambridge, Mass.: Council on East Asian Studies, Harvard University, 1984.

8 The fullest documentation may be found in the six-volume *Yapian zhanzheng* (The Opium War). Edited by Qi Sihe, et al. for the Chinese Historical Society, Shanghai: Shenzhou guoguang she, 1954. A much-admired film about Lin Zexu was made in Shanghai and the film script published in 1961. The fullest biography published in Taiwan was that by Lin Chong-yong in 1968 (Taipei: Commercial Press) and that by Lin's fellow-Fujianese, the historian Yang Guozhen of Xiamen University, in 1981 (Beijing: People's Publishing House). In addition, Lin's poetry, calligraphy, letters, diary were collected and

published in his complete works in 1962. He is the one
mandarin hero of the nineteenth century admired on
both sides of the Straits of Taiwan till this day.

9 Mao Haijian, *Tianchao de bengkui: yapian zhanzheng zai
yanjiu* (The Collapse of the Heavenly Dynasty: a re-
examination of the Opium War). Beijing: Sanlian (Joint
Publishing), 1995. In the 1930s, under the Guomindang regime in Nanjing, Jiang Tingfu (Chiang T'ing-
fu) had thrown doubt about Lin Zexu's understanding of the British in his *Zhongguo jindai shi* (History
of Modern China. Shanghai: Yiwen Research Society, 1938). This drew on his reading of British Foreign
Office sources which he published in two volumes in
1931–1934 (Shanghai: Commercial Press). Mao Haijian
read even more widely, drawing also on Jiang's work,
together with many others who had combed Chinese
and Western sources, and asked more sensitive questions.
Thus his views went much further by pursuing the extent and depth of Lin Zexu's awareness of the military
realities of the time. He concluded that there was no
evidence, even afterwards, that Lin had learnt anything
from his defeat by British naval forces. Mao's views, and
especially his aggressive writing style, did not win him
any favours with the authorities in the Academy. He
was advised to revise some of the strong criticisms in
the book. But he persisted and the book was eventually selected by a distinguished panel of historians who
recommended its publication in the Harvard–Yenching
Academic Library Series published by Joint Publishing
in Beijing.

10 David Pong, *Shen Pao-chen and China's Modernization in
the Nineteenth Century*. Cambridge: Cambridge University Press, 1994, pp. 134–244. Compare with Robert
Hart's own words, "I want to make China strong, and

I want to make England her best friend". In Fairbank, ed. *Cambridge History*, p. 516.

11 Pong, *Shen Pao-chen*, p. 224.

12 Chi Zhonghu, "Haijun dashiji" (Major events concerning the Navy), compiled in 1918 and collected in *Zhongguo jinbainianshi ziliao xubian* (Documents of the recent Hundred Years of Chinese History, Second volume), a selection of documents edited by Zuo Shunsheng. First published in Shanghai by Chung Hua Book company in 1933. The edition used here is the Shanghai reprint of 1996, in the series, Books of the Republican Period. Shanghai: Shanghai Book Company. Fifth series, volume 66, pp. 323–363. This and other contemporary documents are examined in John L. Rawlinson, *China's Struggle for Naval Development, 1839–1895*. Cambridge, Mass.: Harvard University Press, 1967.

13 Rawlinson, *China's Struggle*, pp. 167–197; Swanson, *Eighth Voyage of the Dragon*, pp. 103–112. Also Pao Tsunpeng, *Zhongguo haijun* (China's Navy). Taipei: Hai chün chu pan she, 1951.

14 Yan Fu's preface to the first publication of Chi Zonghu's "Haijun dashiji", reproduced in Zuo Shunsheng's collection, pp. 323–324.

15 Two contrasting approaches are the contemporary work of A. H. Smith, *China in Convulsion*. New York: Revell, 1901, and the recent analytical studies by Joseph W. Esherick, *The Origins of the Boxer Uprising*. Berkeley: University of California Press, 1987, and Paul A. Cohen. *History in Three Keys: the Boxers as event, experience, and myth*. New York: Columbia University Press, 1997. For the lessons of not having a strong navy, see Swanson, *Eighth Voyage of the Dragon*, pp. 113–125.

16 The original research for this development was done by Saneto Keishu before the Second World War. The best

known is his *Nippon bunka no Shina e no eikyo* (Japanese cultural influences on China). Tokyo: Keisetsu Shoin, 1940, pp. 3–39.

17 Jerome Ch'en, *Yuan Shih-kai*. Stanford: Stanford University Press, 1972. Second Edition; James E. Sheridan, *China in Disintegration: the Republican era in Chinese history, 1912–1949*. New York: Free Press, 1975; Lucian Pye, *Warlord Politics: conflict and coalition in the modernization of republican China*. New York: Praeger, 1971.

18 Harold Z. Schriffin, *Sun Yat-sen and the Origins of the Chinese Revolution*. Berkeley: University of California Press, 1968; C. Martin Wilbur, *Sun Yat-sen: frustrated patriot*. New York: Columbia University Press, 1976; J. Y. Wong. *The Origins of an Heroic Image: Sun Yatsen in London, 1896–1897*. Hong Kong: Oxford University Press, 1986.

19 Sun Yat-sen's activities among the Overseas Chinese are well documented in many of the biographical studies about him. The fullest study of his years in British Malaya is the work by Yen Ching-hwang, *The Overseas Chinese and the 1911 Revolution, with special reference to Singapore and Malaya*. Kuala Lumpur: Oxford University Press, 1976. Other studies trace his impact on later and more radical politics among these Chinese; C. F. Yong and R. B. McKenna, *The Kuomintang Movement in British Malaya, 1912–1949*. Singapore: Singapore University Press, 1990; and C. F. Yong, *The Origins of Malayan Communism*. Singapore: South Seas Society, 1997.

The British were also aware of Sun's influence in Canada and the United States. Although less alarming, the growth of a strong following among his Cantonese countrymen greatly concerned the authorities in Hong Kong and various southern Treaty Ports; L. Eve Armentrout-Ma, *Chinese Politics in the Western Hemisphere, 1893–1911: rivalry between reformers and revolutionaries in the Americas*. PhD Thesis, University of California, Davis, 1977. Ann Arbor, Mi.: University Microfilms International. This was revised and published as *Revolutionaries, Monarchists, and Chinatowns: Chinese politics in the Americas and the 1911 Revolution*. Honolulu: University of Hawaii Press, 1990.

20 For Japan, the most authoritative work is still that of Marius B. Jansen, *The Japanese and Sun Yat-sen*. Cambridge, Mass.: Harvard University Press, 1967, 1954.

21 C. Martin Wilbur and Julie Lien-ying How, *Missionaries of Revolution: Soviet Advisers and Nationalist China, 1920–1927*. Cambridge, Mass.: Harvard University Press, 1989; Benjamin I. Schwartz, *Chinese Communism and the Rise of Mao*. Cambridge: Harvard University Press, 1951.

22 Nevertheless, Sa Zhenbing is much admired by his compatriots in Fuzhou; Wang Zhilun and Gao Xiang, *Sa Zhenbing* (Biography of Sa Zhenbing). Fuzhou: Fujian Educational Publishers, 1988; Swanson, *Eighth Voyage of the Dragon*, pp. 113–166.

23 For the military before 1949, the early work of Evans Carlson, *The Chinese Army: its organisation and military efficiency*, is still useful. This was published by the Institute of Pacific Relations in New York in 1940. Also authoritative for this period is F. F. (Frederick Fu) Liu, *A Military History of Modern China, 1924–1949*. Princeton: Princeton University Press, 1956. The background to the full modernisation story, the numerous efforts to train a modern army, can be found in Liu Feng-han's four-volume work, *Xin jun zhi* (History of the New Army). Nangang, Taibei: Institute of Modern History, Academia Sinica, 1967.

24 Chalmers A. Johnson, *Peasant Nationalism and Communist Power: the emergence of revolutionary China, 1937–1945*. Stanford: Stanford University Press, 1962;

Dick Wilson, *The Long March, 1935: the epic of Chinese communism's survival*. London: Hamish Hamilton, 1971.

25 Barbara W. Tuchman, *Sand against the Wind: Stilwell and the American experience in China, 1911–45*. London: Macmillan, 1971. Set against the Stilwell point of view are those of Anna Chennault and Madam Chiang Kai-shek which record China's appreciation of the US factor in the war; Anna Chennault, *Chennault and the Flying Tigers*. New York: P. S. Eriksson, 1963; and Chiang Soong Mei-ling, *This is Our China*, New York and London: Harper & Brothers, 1940. Second edition.

26 Swanson, *Eighth Voyage of the Dragon*, pp. 179–192; eds Yang Guoyu et al., *Dangdai Zhongguo haijun* (The Navy in Contemporary China). Beijing: Zhongguo she-hui kexue (Chinese Social Science) Publishers, 1987, pp. 10–34, 155–223. The defection of the cruiser *Chungking* (originally HMS *Aurora*) was significant. It was manned by British-trained officers who sailed the ship back to China in 1948. The cruiser sailed from Wusong (Shanghai) to Yantai (Shandong) on 25 February 1949. This was followed by the surrender of the Second Fleet in Nanjing in April. Altogether, after sifting out those thought unsuitable, over 4,000 officers and sailors were retained in the PLA's navy. But it was not until 1955 that the PLA was able to recover all islands off the coast, except for those of Mazu and Jinmen and the Pescadores closer to Taiwan.

27 Malcolm H. Murfett, *Hostage on the Yangtze: Britain, China, and the Amethyst crisis of 1949*. Annapolis, Md.: Naval Institute Press, 1991, pp. 50–60, 213–236. The Communists believed that the British had sent naval forces to block the PLA from crossing the Yangzi river and therefore fired their guns at all British vessels, Huang Gangzhou, *Zhang Aiping yu haijun* (Zhang Aiping and the Navy). Beijing: Haichao, 1991, pp. 33–34.

28 Yang et al., *Dangdai Zhongguo haijun*, pp. 47–49, 68–83.

29 Donald S. Zagoria, *The Sino-Soviet Conflict, 1956–1961*. Princeton, N.J.: Princeton University Press, 1962. William E. Griffith, *The Sino-Soviet Rift*. London: Allen & Unwin, 1964.

30 The ramifications of these developments are yet to be fully studied. Two essays by You Ji outline some of the immediate questions that arise: "Missile Diplomacy and PRC domestic politics", in *Missile Diplomacy and Taiwan's Future*. Edited by Greg Austin. Canberra: Strategic and Defence Studies Centre, Australian National University. Canberra Papers on Strategy and Defence, no. 122, 1997, pp. 29–55; and "A Blue Water Navy, does it matter?" in *China Rising: Nationalism and Interdependence*. Edited by David S. G. Goodman and Gerry Segal. London and New York: Routledge, 1997, pp. 71–89.

31 For a background to the skills and interests of the ocean-going Hokkiens, Wang Gungwu, "Merchants Without Empire: the Hokkien sojourning communities", in James D. Tracy ed. *The Rise of Merchant Empires: long-distance trade in the early modern world, 1350–1750*. Cambridge: Cambridge University Press, pp. 400–421.

3 "To trade"

1 Wang Gungwu, *The Chinese Overseas: from earthbound China to the Quest for Autonomy*. Cambridge, Mass.: Harvard University Press, 2000, pp. 24–37; and "Merchants without empires: the Hokkien sojourning communities". In James D. Tracy, ed. *The Rise of Merchant Empires: long-distance trade in the early modern world, 1350–1750*. Cambridge: Cambridge University Press, 1990, pp. 400–421.

2 Edward H. Schafer, "The History of the Empire of Southern Han according to chapter 65 of the *Wu Tai*

shih of Ouyang Hsiu", Silver Jubilee volume of the *Jimbun Kagaku Kenkyujo*, (Kyoto), 1954, pp. 339ff; and *The Empire of Min*. Rutland, Vt.: C. E. Tuttle, for Harvard Yenching Institute, 1954.

3 Carl Crow, *Four Hundred Million Customers: the experiences – some happy, some sad – of an American in China, and what they taught him*. New York: Harper, 1937.

4 S. Gordon Redding, *The Spirit of Chinese Capitalism*. Berlin: W. de Gruyter, 1990. Hao Yen-p'ing, *The Comprador in Nineteenth Century China: bridge between East and West*. Cambridge, Mass.: Harvard University Press, 1970. Albert Feuerwerker, *China's Early Industrialization, Sheng Hsuan-Huai, 1844–1916 and Mandarin enterprise*. Cambridge, Mass.: Harvard University Press, 1958.

5 Wang Gungwu, "The culture of Chinese merchants". In *China and the Chinese Overseas*. Singapore: Times Academic Press, 1991, pp. 188–197.

6 John Keay. *The Honourable Company: a history of the English East India Company*. London: HarperCollins, 1993, pp. 331–361; 421–456.

7 Yu Ying-shih, *Trade and Expansion in Han China: a study in the structure of Sino-barbarian economic relations*. Berkeley: University of California Press, 1967.

8 John K. Fairbank, ed. *The Chinese World Order: Traditional China's foreign relations*. Cambridge, Mass.: Harvard University Press, 1968, pp. 1–14. Fairbank had started in 1941 with research on the Chinese tributary system. This recognised the ancient connection with trade and, while his work evolved into the idea of a Chinese world order, how the system was equally rooted in the feudal politics of official trade was never neglected. That first study was done together with Teng Ssu-yu, "On the Ch'ing Tributary System", *Harvard Journal of Asiatic Studies*, vol. 6, pp. 238–243. Since then, the trade factor has been played down and the tributary system has

been subsumed under that of defence and even "grand strategy". The most recent of such studies are Alastair Iain Johnston, *Cultural Realism: Strategic Culture and Grand Strategy in Chinese History*. Princeton: Princeton University Press, 1995; and Michael D. Swaine and Ashley J. Tellis, *Interpreting China's Grand Strategy: Past, Present, and Future*. Santa Monica, Ca.: Rand, 2000.

Another approach links an extension of the tributary system directly to the characteristics and frequency of war, and goes as far as to call it "the Confucian international order"; Lee Choon Kun, "War in the Confucian International Order". PhD Thesis, University of Texas at Austin, 1988. Ann Arbor, Mi.: University Microfilms International.

9 Frederic Wakeman, jr, "The Canton Trade and the Opium War" in John K. Fairbank ed. *The Cambridge History of China. Volume 10. Late Ch'ing, 1800–1911, Part I*. Cambridge: Cambridge University Press, 1978, pp. 163–171. Cheong Weng Eang, *The Hong Merchants of Canton: Chinese merchants in Sino-Western trade*. London: Curzon Press, 1997, pp. 1–25.

10 F. W. Mote, *Imperial China, 900–1800*. Cambridge, Mass.: Harvard University Press, 1999, pp. 949–956.

11 Wang Gungwu. *The Nanhai Trade*, pp. 116–117; Yang Lien-sheng, "Historical notes on the Chinese world order"; and Marc Mancall, "The Ch'ing tributary system: an interpretative essay", in Fairbank, ed. *The Chinese World Order*, pp. 20–33; 63–85.

12 Morris Rossabi, *Khubilai Khan: his life and times*. Berkeley: University of California Press, 1987, pp. 99–103; 207–220.

13 Ma Huan, *Ying-yai sheng-lan, "The Overall Survey of the Ocean's shores"* [1433]. Translated by J. G. V. Mills. Cambridge: Cambridge University Press for the Hakluyt Society, 1970, pp. 5–34.

14 Ng Chin Keong, "Gentry-Merchants and Peasant-Peddlers – the responses of the South Fukienese to the offshore trading opportunities, 1522–1566", *Nanyang University Journal*, no. 7, 1973, pp. 161–175. Also his *Trade and Society: the Amoy network on the China coast, 1683–1735*. Singapore: Singapore University Press, 1983.

15 James Chin Kong, "Merchants and other sojourners: the Hokkiens overseas, 1570–1760". University of Hong Kong, PhD Thesis, 1999, chapter VII, pp. 316–357. Also Aloysius Chang, "The Chinese community of Nagasaki in the first century of the Tokugawa Period (1603–1688)". St John's University, PhD Thesis, 1970. Ann Arbor, Mich.: University Microfilms International, 1970; and John E. Wills, jr, *Pepper, Guns, and Parleys: the Dutch East India Company and China, 1622–1681*. Cambridge, Mass.: Harvard University Press, 1974, pp. 17–36, 194–212.

16 Jennifer W. Cushman, *Fields from the Sea: Chinese junk trade with Siam during the late eighteenth and early nineteenth centuries*. Ithaca, N.Y.: Cornell Studies on Southeast Asia no. 12, Cornell University, 1993, pp. 65–95; W. L. Schurz, *The Manila Galleon*. New York: Dutton, 1939.

17 Hao Yen-p'ing, *The Commercial Revolution in Nineteenth-Century China: the rise of Sino-Western Mercantile Capitalism*. Berkeley, Ca.: University of California Press, 1986, pp. 17–19.

18 Hao, *Commercial Revolution*, pp. 20–33. During the two decades before the First Opium War, the British merchants reached a position when they outdid all the other foreign merchants seeking to compete off the coast of China.

19 Susan Mann Jones and Philip A. Kuhn, "Dynastic Decline and the Roots of Rebellion", Fairbank ed., *Cambridge History, Late Ch'ing*, pp. 108–132. Robert

P. Gardella, "Qing Administration of the Tea Trade", and Andrea McElderry, "Guarantors and Guarantees in Qing Government-business Relations", in *To Achieve Security and Wealth: the Qing imperial state and the economy, 1644–1911.* Edited by Jane K. Leonard and John R. Watt. Ithaca, N.Y.: East Asia Program, Cornell University, 1992, pp. 97–118; 119–137.

20 Leonard Blussé, "The VOC and the Junk Trade to Batavia: a problem in administrative control", in *Strange Company: Chinese settlers, Mestizo women, and the Dutch in VOC Batavia.* Dordrecht-Holland: Foris Publications, 1988, pp. 97–155; Dianne Lewis, *Jan Campagnie in the Straits of Malacca, 1641–1795.* Athens, Ohio: Ohio University, Center for International Studies, 1995. Reinout Vos, *Gentle Janus, Merchant Prince: the VOC and the tightrope of diplomacy in the Malay world, 1740–1800.* Translated by Beverly Jackson. Leiden: KITLV, 1993. For Manila and the Sulu region, see Nicholas P. Cushner ed., *Documents Illustrating the British Conquest of Manila, 1762–1763.* London: Royal Historical Society, University College, London, 1971. Howard T. Fry, *Alexander Dalrymple (1737–1808) and the expansion of British trade.* Toronto: University of Toronto Press, 1970.

21 J. William Skinner, *Chinese Society in Thailand: an analytical history.* Ithaca, N.Y.: Cornell University Press, 1957; and his *Leadership and Power in the Chinese Community of Thailand.* Ithaca, N.Y.: Published for the Association for Asian Studies by Cornell University Press, 1958. For early Penang and Singapore, K. G. Tregonning, *The British in Malaya: the first forty years, 1786–1826.* Tucson: University of Arizona Press, 1965; and C. M. Turnbull, *The Straits Settlements, 1826–67: Indian presidency to crown colony.* London: Athlone Press, 1972.

22 Wang Dahai (Ong Tae-hae), *Haidao yizhi. The Chinaman Abroad, or, A desultory account of the Malayan Archipelago, particularly of Java.* Translation from the original by

W. H. Medhurst. Shanghai: The Mission Press, 1849. An annotated edition of the original text by Yao Nan and Wu Liangxuan was published in 1992: *Haidao yizhi*. Hong Kong: Xuejin Book Company, Rare Texts Series on the History of the Chinese Overseas, Chinese University of Hong Kong and Huaqiao History Association of Shanghai.

23 The voluminous correspondence that Sheng Xuanhuai has left us reveals the difficulties faced by mandarin entrepreneurs during this transitional period; *Sheng Xuanhuai shiye handian gao* (Sheng Xuanhuai's letters and telegraphs on modern industry in the late Ch'ing period). Edited by Wang Er min and Wu Lun Nixia. Taipei: Academia Sinica Institute of Modern History Documents Series, Two volumes. No. 17, 1993. For a more successful and different kind of literati industrialist, see Samuel C. Chu. *Reformer in Modern China: Chang Chien, 1853–1926*. New York: Columbia University Press, 1965.

24 Parks M. Coble, *The Shanghai Capitalists and the Nationalist Government, 1927–1937*. Cambridge, Mass.: Council on East Asian Studies, Harvard University, 1980, 1986; Sherman Cochran, *Encountering Chinese Networks: Western, Japanese, and Chinese corporations in China, 1880–1937*. Berkeley, Ca.: University of California Press, 2000.

25 Hao Yen-p'ing, *The Comprador in Nineteenth Century China*, pp. 44–63, 207–223; Wellington K. Chan, *Merchants, Mandarins, and Modern Enterprise in Late Ching China*. Cambridge, Mass.: East Asian Research Center, 1977.

26 J. Panglaykim (Pangestu) and I. Palmer, *Entrepreneurship and Commercial Risk: the case of a Schumpeterian business in Indonesia*. Singapore: Institute of Business Studies, Nanyang University, 1970. For Sincere and Wing On

companies, see W. K. Chan, "The origins and early years of the Wing On Company group in Australia, Fiji, Hong Kong and Shanghai: organisation and strategy of a new enterprise", in *Chinese Business Enterprise in Asia*. Edited by Ampalavanar Rajeswary Brown. London: Routledge, 1995, pp. 80–95.

27 Wong Siu-lun, *Emigrant Entrepreneurs: Shanghai industrialists in Hong Kong*. Hong Kong: Oxford University Press, 1988.

28 Redding, *Spirit of Chinese capitalism*, pp. 205–225; 227–240.

29 Yoshihara Kunio, *The Rise of Ersatz Capitalism in South-East Asia*. Singapore: Oxford University Press, 1988.

30 Wong Siu-lun, "The Chinese family firm: a model", *British Journal of Sociology*, vol. 36, no. 1, 1985, pp. 58–72. S. Gordon Redding and G. Y. Y. Wong, "The psychology of Chinese organisational behaviour" in *The Psychology of the Chinese People*. Edited by Michael H. Bond. Hong Kong: Oxford University Press, 1986, pp. 267–295.

31 The best-known examples of centres that were credited with successfully marrying social science teaching with business methods were St John's University in Shanghai and Lingnan University in Guangzhou; Mary Lamberton, *St. John's University, Shanghai, 1879–1951*. New York: United Board for Christian Colleges in China, 1955; Charles Corbett, *Lingnan University, a short history based primarily on the records of the university's American trustees*. New York: Trustees of Lingnan University, 1963.

32 Yong Ching Fatt, *Tan Kah Kee: the making of an overseas Chinese legend*. Singapore: Oxford University Press, 1987, pp. 41–78.

33 Full accounts of Li Ka-shing's life are those in Chinese. The more accessible are Lu Yanyuan, *Li Jiacheng*. Beijing:

Xinhua chubanshe, 1996; and Sun Heping, *Li Jiacheng*.
Jinan: Shandong huabao chubanshe, 1998.

34 Three works by Goh Keng Swee: *The Economics of
Modernization*. Singapore: Federal Publications, 1995;
"Experience & prospect of Singapore's economic development: strategy formulation & execution". Paper
prepared for the Hao Ran Foundation Workshop held
in Macau, from 26 July 1992 to 4 August 1992; and *The
Practice of Economic Growth*. Singapore: Federal Publications, 1977.

35 Edmund Terence Gomez and K. S. Jomo, *Malaysia's
Political Economy: politics, patronage, and profits*. Cambridge
and New York: Cambridge University Press, 1997;
Edmund Terence Gomez, *Chinese Business in Malaysia:
accumulation, ascendance, accommodation*. Richmond,
Surrey: Curzon, 1999.

4 *"To convert"*

1 Holmes Welch, *The Practice of Chinese Buddhism*. Cambridge, Mass.: Harvard University Press, 1967; Erik
Zurcher, *The Buddhist Conquest of China: the spread and
adaptation of Buddhism in early medieval China*. Leiden:
Brill, 1959.

2 Brian Harrison, *Waiting for China: the Anglo-Chinese College at Malacca, 1818–1843, and early nineteenth-century
missions*. Hong Kong: Hong Kong University Press,
1979; Jack S. Gregory, *Great Britain and the Taipings*.
London: Routledge & K. Paul, 1969; Jonathan D.
Spence, *God's Chinese Son: the Taiping Heavenly Kingdom
of Hong Xiuquan*. New York: W. W. Norton, 1996.

3 Paul Cohen, "Christian missions and their impact to
1900". In John K. Fairbank, *The Cambridge History
of China, vol. 10, Late Ch'ing, 1800–1911, Part I*,
pp. 543–590. An excellent essay on the work of James

Legge is Yu Ying-shih's Honorary degrees Convocation Lecture at the University of Hong Kong on 3 October 1992. For *Wanguo gongbao*, see Adrian A. Bennett's *Research Guide to the Wanguo gongbao (The Globe Magazine), 1874–1883*. San Francisco: Chinese Materials Center, 1976.

4 Saneto Keishu, *Chugokujin Nihon ryugaku shi, zoho* (History of Chinese students in Japan), Chinese translation by Tan Ruqian (Tam Yue-him) and Lin Qiyan (Lam Kai-yin). Beijing: Sanlian Joint Publications, 1983.

5 Douglas R. Reynolds, *China, 1898–1912: the Xinzheng revolution and Japan*. Cambridge, Mass.: Council on East Asian Studies, Harvard University, 1993, pp. 1–14; 111–126. *China, 1895–1912: state-sponsored reforms & China's late-Qing revolution*. Selected essays from *Zhongguo Jindai Shi* (Modern Chinese History, 1840–1919). Edited by Douglas R. Reynolds. Armonk, N.Y.: M. E. Sharpe, 1995.

6 As propounded by the generation of Wei Yuan and the early reformers like Li Hongzhang and Zuo Zongtang; Mary Wright, *The Last Stand of Chinese Conservatism: the T'ung-chih Restoration, 1862–1874*. Revised edition. New York: Atheneum, 1966.

7 W. G. Beasley, *Japanese Imperialism, 1894–1945*. Oxford: Clarendon Press, 1987, pp. 108–121; Morinosuke Kajima, *The Diplomacy of Japan, 1894–1922*. Tokyo: Kajima Institute of International Peace, 1976–1980. Vol. 3, pp. 126ff.

8 Saneto Keishu, *Chugokujin Nihon ryugaku shi* pp. 281–338.

9 Chang Hao, *Chinese Intellectuals in Crisis: search for order and meaning (1890–1911)*. Berkeley, Ca.: University of California Press, 1987, his concluding remarks on four leading intellectuals, pp. 181–191.

10 Wen Ching (Lim Boon Keng), *The Chinese Crisis from Within*. Edited by G. M. Reith. London: Library of Congress, 1901. Lee Guan Kin (Li Yuanjin), *Lin Wenqing di sixiang: Zhongxi wenhua di huiliu yu maodun* (The ideas of Lim Boon Keng: convergence and contradiction between Chinese and Western culture). Singapore: Singapore Society for Asian Studies, 1990, pp. 78–86.

11 Adrian A. Bennett, *John Fryer: the introduction of Western science and technology into nineteenth-century China*. Cambridge, Mass.: East Asian Research Center, Harvard University, 1967; Paul R. Bohr, *Famine in China and the Missionary: Timothy Richard as relief administrator and advocate of national reform, 1876–1884*. Cambridge, Mass.: East Asian Research Center, Harvard University, 1972. W. A. P. Martin, *The Lore of Cathay; or, the intellect of China*. New York, Chicago: Fleming H. Revell, 1901; and *Hanlin Papers: or, Essays on the intellectual life of the Chinese*. London: Trubner, 1880.

12 Liu T'ieh-yun (Liu E), *The Travels of Lao Ts'an*. Translated by Harold Shadick. New York: Columbia University Press, 1990 (fist published by Ithaca, N.Y.: Cornell University Press, 1952), pp. xix–xxv; 3–11.

13 Chen Tingzhuo, *Baiyu zhai cihua* (*Ci*-poetry notes from the White Rain Studio). First edited and published in a traditional wood-cut edition in 1894 by my great-grandfather, Wang Gengxin, in eight chapters. This was reprinted in modern type by Kai-ming Publishers in Shanghai in the 1930s. A punctuated edition was published in Beijing by Wenxue guji kanxingshe in 1959. Chen's complete manuscript in ten chapters was photographically reprinted in Shanghai by Guji chubanshe in 1984, together with his anthology of ci-poetry, *Ci Ze* (Patterns of *Ci*-poetry).

Ding Chuanjing (Ting Ch'uan-ching) was known after 1911 for his novels and even better known when his collection of poems was published after his death in 1930. His *Songren yishi huibian* (first edition published in Shanghai by Commercial Press in 1935) was translated by Djang Chu and Jane C. Djang, *A Compilation of Anecdotes of Sung Personalities*. Taipei: St. John's University Press, 1989.

14 Vera Schwarcz, *The Chinese Enlightenment: intellectuals and the legacy of the May Fourth Movement of 1919*. Berkeley, Ca.: University of California Press, 1986, pp. 94–144; Lin, Yu-sheng, *The Crisis of Chinese Consciousness: Radical antitraditionalism in the May Fourth era*. Madison: University of Wisconsin Press, 1979; Benjamin I. Schwartz, ed. *Reflections on the May Fourth Movement: a symposium*. Cambridge, Mass.: East Asian Research Center, Harvard University, 1972.

15 Taylor, Mrs Howard (M. Geraldine Guinness), *The Story of the China Inland Mission*. With an introduction by J. Hudson Taylor. London: Morgan & Scott, 1900. Two volumes; A. J. Broomhall, *Hudson Taylor & China's Open Century*. Sevenoaks, Kent: Hodder and Stoughton and the Overseas Missionary Fellowship, 1981; Paul R. Bohr, *Famine in China and the Missionary;* Howard Taylor, *Hudson Taylor in Early Years: the growth of a soul*. Singapore: Overseas Missionary Fellowship, 1989 (Original edition, 1911).

16 Pat Barr, *To China with Love: the lives and times of Protestant missionaries in China 1860–1900*. London: Secker and Warburg, 1972; John Leighton Stuart, *Fifty Years in China: the memoirs of John Leighton Stuart, missionary and ambassador*. New York: Random House, 1954: James B. Webster, *Christian Education and the National Consciousness in China*. New York: E. P. Dutton, 1923.

17 John Wong, *The Origins of an Heroic Image: Sun Yatsen in London, 1896–1897*. Hong Kong: Oxford University Press, pp. 169–202. Harold Z. Schriffin, *Sun Yat-sen*

and the Origins of the Chinese Revolution. Berkeley, Ca.: University of California Press, 1968.

18 Victor Purcell, *Problems of Chinese Education*. London: K. Paul, Trench, Trubner, 1936; Gwee Yee Hean and Francis H. K. Wong, *Official Reports on Education: the Straits Settlements and the Federated Malay States, 1870–1939*. Singapore: Pan Pacific Book Distributors, 1980.

19 Lin Shu's translations in classical Chinese prose include works like Lamb's *Tales from Shakespeare, Robinson Crusoe, Gulliver's Travels*, and the major novels of Charles Dickens. There were also innumerable contemporary popular novels from Britain, most notably those of H. Rider Haggard and Arthur Conan Doyle, but few of these are read today in China. The best of the English and French classical novels were later re-translated by others into *baihua* for a wider audience. Selections of Lin Shu's own prose and poetry have been recently reprinted to illustrate the influence he had on his times. The most representative of these is the collection, *Lin Shu yanjiu ziliao* (Research materials on Lin Shu). Fuzhou: Fujian People's Publishing House, 1983. Lin Shu's advocacy of classical Chinese is recalled through his scholarly writings and reprints of his selections of traditional prose essays.

20 Howard L. Boorman, ed. *Biographical Dictionary of Republican China*. vol. 2, pp. 122–124 (Xu Zhimo); vol. 3, pp. 132–135 (Lao She, or Shu Qingchun); vol. 2, pp. 148–149 (Xu Dishan). Xiao Qian does not have a biography, but is mentioned in several articles, notably as a victim of the anti-Rightist campaign of 1957, vol. 3, p. 357. There are innumerable studies of Xu Zhimo, especially his poetry. Zhu Guangqian's biography by Qian Niansun, *Zhu Guangqian yu Zhongxi wenhua* (Zhu Guangqian and China-West culture). Hefei: Anhui jiaoyu chubanshe, 1995.

21 *Zhu Guangqian quanji* (Complete Works). Hefei: Anhui jiaoyu chubanshe, 1987, vol. 9, p. 186.

22 "Gei qingnian di shierfeng xin (Twelve Letters to the Young)". In Zhu, *Complete Works*, vol. 1, pp. 1–81.

23 Waley, "A Debt to China". In Hsiao Ch'ien (comp.), *A Harp with a Thousand Strings*, p. 342.

24 G. Lowes Dickinson's *The Greek View of Life* (first published in London by Methuen in 1896) was translated and published in 1934 by Shanghai Commercial Press, and reprinted in Taipei in 1966. The English original of this work was available in major Chinese universities. The major texts of the Greek classics were translated into Chinese between 1900 and 1930 and scholars were familiar with them. It is interesting that the most detailed study of the Greek city-states written since 1949 does not refer to Dickinson; Gu Zhun, "Xila bangcheng zhidu" (The Greek city-state system), in *Gu Zhun wenji* (The works of Gu Zhun), Guiyang: Guizhou People's Publishing, 1994, pp. 63–219. As for Dickinson's later book, *An Essay on the Civilisations of India, China and Japan* (published in London by J. M. Dent in 1914), that was also available in China. I am not aware, however, whether his books became better known because of his visit to China and the Chinese friends he made there. His very successful *Letters from John Chinaman*, first published in 1901, also by Dent in London, does not seem to have been known in China.

25 Bertrand Russell, *The Problem of China*, London: Allen & Unwin, 1966 (first published in 1922); translated as *Zhongguo wenti* by Qin Yue. Shanghai: Xuelin chubanshe, 1996. Some of the notes based on Russell's lectures in China were subsequently published during the years 1922–1926. Recent Chinese writings about Russell have referred to his articles about China published in newspapers and magazines between 1921 and 1927. This

is brought out in Li Xueqin's review in *Dushu* maga-
zine, no. 1 of 1996 (Beijing) of Feng Chongyi's study of
Russell and China, *Luosu yu Zhongguo*. Beijing: Sanlian
Joint Publishing, 1994.

26 Translated by Hsu Kai-yu in *Twentieth Century Chinese
Poetry: an anthology*. Garden City, N.Y.: Doubleday,
1963, pp. 83–84. Also in Cyril Birch, ed. *Anthology of
Chinese Literature. Vol. 2: From the 14ᵗʰ century to the present
day*. New York: Grove Press, 1972, pp. 347–348.

27 Xiao Qian, *Weidai ditu de luren: Xiao Qian huiyi lu* (Memoirs of Xiao Qian). Hong Kong: Xiangjiang Publishers, 1988. This was abridged, adapted and translated by
Jeffrey C. Kinkley, and expanded and revised by Xiao
Qian, as *Traveler without a Map*. London: Hutchinson,
1990, chapters 1 to 3. In Mao's China, Xiao began as
a deputy chief editor of the English edition of *Renmin
Zhongguo* (People's China). In order to test his loyalty, he
was asked to be one of the editors of the *Literature and
Art Gazette* and adviser to the literary section of *Renmin
Ribao* (People's Daily), both controlled by the Communist Party. But he had been outspoken in support of a
more liberal view of literature, even going as far as defending translations of D. H. Lawrence, for which he
was not forgiven. Thus his position and reputation did
not save him from persecution as a "Rightist" in 1957.

28 Xiao-Kinkley, *Traveler without a Map*, p. 111.

29 Xiao-Kinkley, *Traveler without a Map*, p. 117.

30 Xiao's first books published in England were *Etching of
a Tormented Age: a glimpse of contemporary Chinese literature*. London: Allen & Unwin, 1940; and *China: but
not Cathay*. London: Pilot Press, 1942. He also translated Charles and Mary Lamb's *Tales from Shakespeare* and
Henry Fielding's *The Life of Jonathan Wild*, both first
published in 1956 before he was disgraced. Although

not allowed to publish, he continued to translate. In 1962, under a pseudonym, he even managed to publish his translations of a selection of Stephen Leacock's satirical essays, *Likeke fenchi xiaopin xuan*. Beijing: People's Publishing. After his rehabilitation in 1979, until his death twenty years later, a flood of his writings appeared. This includes his memoirs and four major translations: Henrik Ibsen's *Peer Gynt* (Chongqing: People's Publishing, 1983), Upton Sinclair's *The Jungle* (Beijing: People's Literature, 1984), Henry Fielding's *The History of Tom Jones* (Beijing: People's Literature, 1984, two volumes) and finally, James Joyce's *Ulysses* (Nanjing: Yilin, 1994, three volumes).

31 Talented writers from China did write and publish in English before the Second World War, but they were mostly scholars, translators, and political commentators. The best known of them was probably Lin Yutang (1895–1976) who was a product of a missionary school in China, the Anglo-Chinese School in Gulangyu, the island opposite Xiamen (Amoy) in Fujian province.

32 Yung Wing, *My Life in China and America*. New York: H. Holt, 1909. Hu Shi (1891–1962) was much respected but wrote far more in Chinese than in English. Another who was highly regarded was Wellington V. K. Koo (1888–1985). He wrote his memoirs in English, but this has only been published in Chinese translation, in ten volumes.

33 Ku Hung-ming and Lim Boon Keng were even more at home in English, but did not have Lin Yutang's deep understanding of Chinese literature and philosophy. Ku Hung-ming is best known for his three books: *Papers from a Viceroy's Yamen: a Chinese plea for the cause of good government and true civilization in China*. Shanghai: Shanghai Mercury, 1901; *The Spirit of the Chinese People: with an*

essay on civilization and anarchy. Peking: Commercial
Press, 1922; *The Story of a Chinese Oxford Movement*.
Shanghai: Shanghai Mercury, 1912.

34 The most influential of his translations were of Adam
Smith (1723–1790), *Inquiry into the Nature and Causes
of the Wealth of Nations* (Yuan fu); John Stuart Mill
(1806–1873), *On Liberty* (Qunji quanjie lun); Herbert
Spencer (1820–1903), *Study of Sociology* (Qunxue yiyan);
Thomas Huxley (1825–1895), *Evolution and Ethics* (Tian
yan lun); Edward Jenks (1861–1939), *History of Politics*
(She hui tong quan); Benjamin I. Schwartz, *In search
of Wealth and Power: Yen Fu and the West*. Cambridge,
Mass.: Belknap Press, 1964, chaps. IV–VIII.

35 Daniel Kwok, *Scientism in Chinese Thought, 1900–1950*.
New Haven: Yale University Press, 1965.

36 Arif Dirlik, *Revolution and History: the origins of Marxist
historiography in China, 1919–1937*. Berkeley, Ca.: University of California Press, 1978. *Dushu zazhi* was published from 1931 vol. 1, no. 1 to 1933 vol. 3, no. 6. Zhao
Qinghe, *Dushu zazhi yu Zhongguo shehuishi lunzhan,
1931–1933* (*Dushu zazhi* and the debate on China's social history, 1931–1933) [Historical Monographs series].
Taipei: Jia Ho Publishing, 1995.

37 Albert Feuerwerker, ed. *History in Communist China*.
Cambridge, Mass.: M.I.T. Press, 1968.

38 The best known were Li Shihzhen (1518–1593), *Bencao gangmu* (The Great Pharmacopoeia); Wang Zhen
(14th century), *Nong shu* (Treatise on Agriculture); Xu
Guangqi (1562–1633), *Nongzheng quanshu* (Complete
Treatise on Agriculture); Song Yingxing (b. 1587) *Tiangong kaiwu* (The Exploitation of the Works of Nature).

    Parts of *Bencao gangmu* were translated into English
as *Chinese Materia Medica*, by Bernard E. Read and
published in Beijing in the *Peking Natural History Bul-
letin* (1931–1941), reprinted in Taipei: Southern Materia

Center, 1977. A recent study is George Metailie, "The *Bencao gangmu* of Li Shihzhen: an innovation in natural history?", in *Innovation in Chinese Medicine*. Edited by Elizabeth Hsu, Cambridge: Cambridge University Press, 2001, pp. 221–261.

W. H. Medhurst translated parts of Xu Guangqi's *Nonzheng quanshu*. This was entitled *Dissertation on the Silk-manufacture, and the Cultivation of the Mulberry*, and published by the Mission Press in Shanghai in 1849. The translation of Song Yingxing's *Tiangong kaiwu* was published as *Chinese Technology in the Seventeenth Century*, by E-tu Zen Sun and Shiou-chuan Sun, University Park: Pennsylvania State University, 1966.

39 The earliest work by Chinese scholars themselves on the history of mathematics, calendrical science, physics and alchemy were Li Nian (1892–1963), Yan Dunjie (1917–1988), Zhu Kezhen (1890–1974), Wang Jin (b. 1895) and Ding Xuxian (1885–1978). In the field of engineering, Liu Xianzhou (1890–1975) graduated from the University of Hong Kong in 1918 and later became vice-president of Qinghua University. He became interested in engineering history in the 1930s and published several studies, which came together as *Zhongguo jixie gongcheng famingshi* (History of Chinese engineering inventions). Beijing: Kexue chubanshe, 1962; and *Zhongguo gudai nongye jixie famingshi* (History of Chinese inventions in agricultural engineering). Beijing: Kexue chubanshe, 1963.

40 Wong Chimin and Wu Lien-teh, *History of Chinese Medicine, being a chronicle of medical happenings in China from ancient times to the present period*. Shanghai: National Quarantine Service, 1936.

41 Joseph Needham, *Science and Civilisation in China*. Cambridge: Cambridge University Press, 1954–. Ho Peng Yoke, *Li, Qi and Shu: an introduction to science and*

civilization in China. Hong Kong: Hong Kong University Press, 1985 and *Wo yü Li Yüeh-se* (I and Joseph Needham). Hong Kong: Joint Publications, 1985.

5 *"To rule"*

1   Biographical data of Chinese elites in the past followed a formula and did not seek to provide a rounded picture of their lives. They mostly recorded the public lives of their subjects but, wherever possible, linkages with family and ancestors were identified. Modern biographies capture the different stages better: for example, Zhu Dongrun's biography of a controversial Prime Minister of the Ming dynasty, *Zhang Juzheng zhuan* (Biography of Zhang Juzheng, 1525–1582). Taipei: Tai-wan kai-ming shu-tien, 1968; and Arthur Waley's biography of Yuan Mei (1716–1798), *Yuan Mei: Eighteenth century Chinese poet*. London: George Allen & Unwin, 1956.

2   The revival of traditional religions among Chinese on the mainland since the Cultural Revolution has been widely noted. Recently, the Communist Party has spoken of the need to recognise the importance of moral and spiritual values for the country; *Gongmin daode jianshe shisi gangyao* (Outline of measures for building public morality), www.peopledaily.com.cn, 24 October 2001. Following the meetings on religious affairs called by the Party and the State Council on 10–12 December 2001, there have been regular reports and editorials on the subject of religion in the *People's Daily* in 2002.

   For Falungong, Benjamin Penny, "Falun gong, Prophesy and Apocalypse", *East Asian History*, no. 23, June 2002, pp. 149–168; John Wong and William T. Liu, *The Mystery of China's Falun Gong: its rise and its sociological implications*. Singapore: World Scientific and Singapore University Press, 1999.

3 This was reported in *Hai Lu* (Record of the Seas), the account based on the experiences of Xie Qinggao who was a sailor during the last decades of the 18th century. Yang Bingnan, *Hai lu*. Shanghai: Shangwu yinshuguan (Commercial Press), 1936.

4 Robert Bickers, *Britain in China: community, culture and colonialism, 1900–1949*. Manchester: Manchester University Press, 1999.

5 Robert Hart was appointed with two other Englishmen, H. Tudor Davies and George Fitzroy, for the period 1861–63, when they held the job in Shanghai. Stanley F. Wright, *Hart and the Chinese Customs*. Belfast: W. Mullan, published for Queen's University, 1950. Juliet Bredon, *Sir Robert Hart: the romance of a great career*. New York: Dutton, 1909. Robert Hart, *The I.G. in Peking: letters of Robert Hart, Chinese Maritime Customs, 1868–1907*. Edited by John King Fairbank, Katherine Frost Bruner, Elizabeth MacLeod Matheson. Cambridge, Mass.: The Belknap Press of Harvard University Press, 1975.

6 John D. Frodsham, *The First Chinese Embassy to the West: the journals of Kuo Sung-Tao, Liu Hsi-Hung and Chang Te-yi*. Oxford: Clarendon Press, 1974; Owen Wong Hong-hin, *A New Profile in Sino-Western diplomacy: the first Chinese Minister to Great Britain*. Kowloon: Zhonghua Book Company, 1987.

7 Hsiao Kung-chuan, *A Modern China and a New World: K'ang Yu-wei, reformer and utopian, 1858–1927*. Seattle: University of Washington Press, 1975; also *K'ang Yu-wei: a biography and a symposium*. Edited, with translation by Lo Jung-pang. Tucson: Published for the Association for Asian Studies by University of Arizona Press, 1967; and Chang Hao, *Liang Ch'i-ch'ao and Intellectual Transition in China, 1890–1907*. Cambridge, Mass.: Harvard University Press, 1971.

8 Schwartz, *In Search of Wealth and Power*, pp. 42–90.
No Chinese scholar before or after Yan Fu devoted
as much energy to the work of British intellectuals;
with one exception, they were all men of the 19th century: Adam Smith, John Stuart Mill, Herbert Spencer,
Thomas Huxley and Edward Jenks.

9 Ernest P. Young, "Politics in the aftermath of revolution: the era of Yuan Shih-k'ai, 1912–16", in *The
Cambridge History of China, volume 12: Republican China,
1912–1949, Part I*. Edited by John K. Fairbank. Cambridge: Cambridge University Press, 1983, pp. 246–255.
Jerome Ch'en, *Yuan Shih-K'ai, 1859–1916: Brutus
assumes the purple*. London: George Allen & Unwin,
1961.

10 Vera Schwarcz, *The Chinese Enlightenment*, pp. 145–194.
Chow Tse-tsung, *The May Fourth Movement: Intellectual
Revolution in Modern China*. Cambridge, Mass.: Harvard
University Press, 1960.

11 Early "Marxist" writings showed the influence of
Japanese communists, who had less trouble with feudalism than the Chinese historians. *Dushu zazhi*, 1931, vol.
1, no. 1–1933, vol. 3, no. 6. Zhao Qing-he, *Dushu zazhi
yu Zhongguo, 1995*. Marian Sawer, *Marxism and the Question of the Asiatic Mode of Production*. The Hague: Nijhoff,
1977. *The Asiatic Mode of Production in China*. Edited by
Timothy Brook. Armonk, N.Y.: M. E. Sharpe, 1989.

12 Russell, *The Problem of China*, pp. 18–20, 146–148.

13 Dewey's lectures in China, mainly on philosophy of
education, were translated and published in Beijing in
1920 and in 1921, and these have been translated back
into English and published in 1973. Dewey himself was
impressed by the warm reception he received; John
Dewey and Alice C. Dewey, *Letters from China and Japan,
1919–1920*. London: Dent, 1920. He has not received
as much attention in recent years as Russell among

scholars in China. David L. Hall and Roger T. Ames, *The Democracy of the Dead: Dewey, Confucius, and the hope for democracy in China*. Chicago, Ill.: Open Court, 1998; Barry C. Keenan, *The Dewey Experiment in China: educational reform and political power in the early Republic*. Cambridge, Mass.: Council on East Asian Studies, Harvard University, 1977.

14 Lin Shu began translating Dickens in the 1910s, including *Oliver Twist*, *David Copperfield*, *Nicholas Nickleby*, *Dombey and Son*, *The Old Curiosity Shop*. Others after him in the 1920s translated *A Christmas Carol*, *Great Expectations*, *Hard Times* and *A Tale of Two Cities*. By that time, the sympathy for the words of William Blake (1757–1827) was also influenced by the approval of Dickens among Russian revolutionaries who considered Dickens as their predecessor in their criticism of capitalist exploitation.

15 George Leith, *A Short Account of the Settlement, Produce and Commerce of Prince of Wales Island in the Straits of Malacca*. London: J. Barfield, 1804. For early Penang and Singapore, C. D. Cowan, "Early Penang and the rise of Singapore, 1805–1832", *Journal of the Malayan Branch of the Royal Asiatic Society*, vol. 23, part 2, 1950, pp. 1–210; Ernest Chew, "The founding of a British settlement", in *A History of Singapore*. Edited by E. C. T. Chew and Edwin Lee. Singapore: Oxford University Press, 1991, pp. 36–40.

16 Edwin Lee, *The British as Rulers: governing multi-racial Singapore, 1867–1914*. Singapore: Singapore University Press, 1991, pp. 50–99. C. M. Turnbull, *A History of Singapore, 1819–1975*. Singapore: Oxford University Press, 1985. The favourable views of the leading Chinese traders would have to be compared with the views of later immigrants, and also with those of the nationalists and revolutionaries, see Lee Poh Ping. *Chinese Society in*

Nineteenth Century Singapore. Kuala Lumpur: University of Malaya Press, 1978; and Yen Ching-hwang, *Community and Politics: the Chinese in colonial Singapore and Malaysia*. Singapore: Times Academic Press, 1995.

17 Mark Elvin, "The administration of Shanghai, 1905–1914", in *The Chinese City between Two Worlds*. Edited by Mark Elvin and G. William Skinner. Stanford: Stanford University Press, 1974, pp. 239–262; Liang Yuen-sheng, *The Shanghai Taotai: linkage man in a changing society, 1843–90*. Honolulu: University of Hawaii Press, 1990; and Marie Claire Bergere, "The role of the bourgeoisie", in *China in Revolution: the first phase, 1900–1913*. Edited by Mary C. Wright. New Haven and London: Yale University Press, 1968, pp. 229–295. An illuminating study of a specific area of urban administration may be found in Kerrie L. MacPherson, *A Wilderness of Marshes: the origins of Public Health in Shanghai, 1843–1893*. Hong Kong: Oxford University Press, 1987.

On the increasingly lively Chinese press, Li Shao-nan, "Xianggang di zhongxi baoye (Chinese and Western newspapers in Hong Kong)". In Wang Gungwu ed. *Xianggang shi xinbian* (Hong Kong History: new perspectives). Vol. 2, pp. 493–533; and Chen Mong Hock, *The Early Chinese Newspapers of Singapore, 1881–1912*. Singapore: University of Malaya Press, 1967.

18 Song Ong Siang, *One Hundred Years of the Chinese in Singapore*. Singapore: University of Malaya Press, 1967 reprint. (First published in London in 1923.) The work was never translated into Chinese, although much of its rich biographical material was included in various collections of biographies published in Chinese. The most recent example is Kua Bak Lim, ed. *Who's Who in the Chinese Community of Singapore*. Singapore: EPB Publishers, 1995. One of the few studies of Song Ong Siang

compares him with two contemporaries who were more prolific than him; Lee Guan Kin (Lee Yuanjin), *Dongxi wenhua de chuangji yu Xinhua zhishifenzhi de sanzhong huiying* (Responding to Eastern and Western Cultures in Singapore: a comparative study of Khoo Seok Wan, Lim Boon Keng and Song Ong Siang). Singapore and River Edge, NJ: Singapore University Press and Global Publishing, 2001. Also see Yong C. F. (Ching Fatt), *Chinese Leadership and Power in Colonial Singapore*. Singapore: Times Academic Press, 1992.

Tan Cheng Lock, *Malayan Problems: from a Chinese point of view*. Edited by C. Q. Lee; with an introduction by Wu Lien-teh. Singapore: Tannsco, 1947. Lim Kean Siew, *The Eye over the Golden Sands: the memoirs of a Penang family*. Petaling Jaya: Pelanduk Publications, 1997.

19 On the futility of Hong Rengan's (Hung Jen-kan) worthy ideals, the views of the Reverend Joseph Edkins in 1861 are telling:

The books are partly explanatory of the religion of the Bible, and partly political. They recommend various improvements in the constitution of the state, the institutions of social life, and in the arts. They describe the advantages of railways, of the electric telegraph, of a post office, of newspapers, and of steam machinery... Unfortunately, these visions of future prosperity are not accompanied by the genius for conquest and for government... They would do better to busy themselves in forming an efficient government for the territory now under their power than to be dreaming of possible improvements when the present era of anarchy shall close.

Quoted in Prescott Clarke and J. S. Gregory, *Western Reports on the Taiping: a selection of documents*. Canberra: Australian National University Press, 1982, pp. 293–294 and 360–361; Jonathan D. Spence, *God's Chinese Son*, pp. 269–273.

20 Tsai Jung-fang, "Syncretism in the reformist thought of Ho Kai and Hu Li-yuan", *Asian Profile*, vol. 6, no. 1, 1978, pp. 19–33; and "The predicament of the comprador ideologists: He Qi and Hu Liyuan", *Modern China*, vol. 7, no. 2, 1981, pp. 191–225.

Paul Cohen, in his essay on Christian missions, describes Zheng Guanying's *Shengshi weiyan* (first published 1893, with expanded editions, most recently collected in *Zheng Guanying ji* (Collected works of Zheng Guanying). Edited by Xia Dongyuan. Two volumes. Beijing, 1982–1988): "the humanitarian sentiments permeating his influential reform tract were clearly of Christian provenance", "Christian Missions and their Impact to 1900". In Fairbank, *Cambridge History of China*, vol. 10, part I, p. 584.

21 Linda Pomerantz-Zhang, *Wu Tingfang, 1842–1922: reform and modernization in modern Chinese history*. Hong Kong: Hong Kong University Press, 1992.

22 Brian Harrison, ed. *University of Hong Kong: the first 50 years, 1911–1961*. Hong Kong: Hong Kong University Press, 1962, pp. 45–57; and Chan Lau Kit-ching and Peter Cunich, *An Impossible Dream: Hong Kong University from Foundation to Re-establishment*. Oxford: Oxford University Press, 2003. The alumni in China produced a volume of essays recalling their experiences at HKU, *Yizhi yiye zongguanqing* (Sentiments in leaf and branch). Edited by Liu Shuyong. Hong Kong: Hong Kong University Press, 1993.

On Liu Xianzhou, pp. 35–51. Also, see *75 years of Engineering: 75th anniversary commemorative publication of the Faculty of Engineering, The University of Hong Kong*. Hong Kong: HKU Faculty of Engineering, 1988.

23 Sun Yat-sen gave his lecture at HKU on 19 February 1923; Sun *Zhongshan quanji* (Complete Works of

Sun Yat-sen), Beijing: Zhonghua Book company, 1985, vol. 7, pp. 115–117. The nostalgia he had for his youthful student days in Hong Kong was greatly different from his deep suspicions about British policies a few years earlier. His views in 1917 are expressed in "The question of China's survival", now confirmed to have been the ideas of Sun and translated in *Prescriptions for Saving China: selected writings of Sun Yat-sen*. Edited by Julie Lee Wei, Ramon H. Myers and Donald G. Gillin. Stanford Ca.: Hoover Institution, 1994, pp. 131–199.

24 Both the community organisations and the social divisions in the Malay States and the Straits Settlements are captured clearly in C. S. Wong, *A Gallery of Chinese Kapitans*. Singapore: Dewan Bahasa dan Kebudayaan, Ministry of Culture, 1963, pp. 9–37, 67–87; and Yen Ching-hwang, *Community and Politics: the Chinese in colonial Singapore and Malaysia*. Singapore: Times Academic Press, 1995, pp. 3–22, 33–53.

25 C. F. Yong, *The Origins of Malayan Communism*. Singapore: South Seas Society, 1997, pp. 241–268; F. Spencer Chapman, *The Jungle is Neutral*. London: Chatto & Windus, 1949.

26 Khoo Kay Kim. The beginnings of political extremism in Malaya, 1915–1935. PhD Thesis. Department of History, University of Malaya, 1975. Cheah Boon Kheng, *Red Star over Malaya: resistance and social conflict during and after the Japanese occupation of Malaya, 1941–1946*. Singapore: Singapore University Press, 1983; and *The Masked Comrades: a study of the communist United Front in Malaya, 1945–48*. Singapore: Times Books International, 1979. Yeo Kim Wah, *Political Development in Singapore, 1945–55*. Singapore: Singapore University Press, 1973.

27 Lee Kuan Yew, *The Singapore Story: Memoirs of Lee Kuan Yew*. Singapore: Times Editions, 1998, pp. 256ff. Also, earlier studies by Alex Josey, *Lee Kuan Yew*. Singapore:

D. Moore Press, 1968; and *Lee Kuan Yew: the crucial years*. Singapore: Times Books International, 1980; John Drysdale, *Singapore: Struggle for Success*. Singapore: Times Books International, 1984.

28 Kuan Hsin-chi and Lau Siu-kai, *Political Attitudes in a Changing Context: the case of Hong Kong*. Hong Kong: Hong Kong Institute of Asia-Pacific Studies, Chinese University of Hong Kong, 1997. Ambrose Y. C. King and Rance P. L. Lee, eds, *Social Life and Development in Hong Kong*. Hong Kong: Chinese University Press, 1981.

29 Ian Scott, *Political Change and the Crisis of Legitimacy in Hong Kong*. London: Hurst, 1989, pp. 127–170; Lui Ting Terry, "Changing civil servants' values", in *The Hong Kong Civil Service and its Future*. Edited by Ian Scott and John P. Burns. Hong Kong: Oxford University Press, 1988, pp. 131–158.

30 Jonathan Dimbleby, *The Last Governor: Chris Patten & the handover of Hong Kong*. Toronto: Doubleday Canada, 1997, pp. 94ff.

31 Alvin Y. So, *Hong Kong's Embattled Democracy: a societal analysis*. Baltimore: Johns Hopkins University Press, 1999; Wang Gungwu and John Wong, eds, *Hong Kong in China: the Challenges of Transition*. Singapore: Times Academic Press, 1999. A close examination of the political and administrative system is found in Yash Ghai, *Hong Kong's New Constitutional Order: the resumption of Chinese Sovereignty and the Basic Law*. Hong Kong: Hong Kong University Press, 1997, pp. 221–280 and 371–427.

6 Beyond Waley's list

1 Waley, "A Debt to China", in *A Harp with a Thousand Strings*, p. 342.

2 Lynn Pan, ed., *Encyclopedia of the Chinese Overseas*. Singapore and Cambridge, Mass.: Chinese Heritage

Centre, Singapore, and Harvard University Press, 1999,
pp. 15–17, 48–71; and M. Jocelyn Armstrong and
R. Warwick Armstrong, "Introduction: Chinese populations of Southeast Asia", in *Chinese Populations in Contemporary Southeast Asian Societies: Identities, Interdependence and International Influence*. Edited by M. Jocelyn
Armstrong, R. Warwick Armstrong and Kent Mulliner.
Richmond, Surrey: Curzon, 2001, pp. 1–10. The total
number of Chinese overseas is a figure difficult to determine or agree on. Most scholars use a figure between 25
and 30 million, but some have claimed the larger figure
of 30 to 35 million. This figure would include some who
might still consider themselves as Chinese sojourners
or overseas Chinese (*huaqiao*, see chapter one, note 3),
but it does not include the Chinese who live in Taiwan,
Hong Kong, and Macau who, if included, would add
another 30 million to the total. Such a figure of 60 million would be totally misleading. From the point of view
of Beijing, Taipei and Chinese communities elsewhere,
the additional 30 million are not included in the term
Haiwai huaren (Chinese overseas).

At this stage, it is still useful to distinguish those Chinese living in Hong Kong and Macau from those who
live in the PRC, although both those territories are now
part of the PRC. The Chinese in Taiwan, however, have
their own state system under the name of the Republic
of China. For them, the official term *huaqiao* (overseas
Chinese) is only used to describe Chinese not living
in Taiwan or on Mainland China. Under the circumstances, it is important to be clear that the "Chinese overseas" refers to Chinese living outside China (or Greater
China) and not outside the PRC.

3 China's encounters with Britain have usually been
wrapped up in a larger blanket of relations with the West.
Two notable studies are Y. C. Wang's *Chinese Intellectuals and the West, 1872–1949*. Chapel Hill: University of

North Carolina Press, 1966, and Jerome Ch'en's *China and the West: Society and Culture, 1815–1937*. London: Hutchinson, 1979. The first pays more attention to the Chinese-American story and the second takes on all of Europe as well. The lectures here focus on Britain and include the Chinese who lived under British jurisdiction. The Chinese who have settled elsewhere in the Commonwealth would need another book.

4 Jiang Zemin's Speech at the 80th anniversary of the Chinese Communist Party on 1 July, *Renmin Ribao* (People's Daily), 2 July 2001.

5 The Chinese Academy of the Social Sciences (CASS) in Beijing has led the way for all its sister academies in the provinces to give greater prominence to the social science divisions recognised and institutionalised in Europe and North America; Qiao Jian, Li Peiliang and Ma Rong, eds, *Shehui kexue de yingyong yu Zhongguo xiandaihua* (Application of Social Sciences and China's Modernization). Beijing: Peking University Press, 1999. This has led to improvements in the way new knowledge is being presented and the changes are appreciated by the policy-making bodies of the national government. A good example is the way annual analyses of China's development have been organised disciplines, now available annually. For example, *Zhongguo jingji qianjing fenxi*. Edited by Liu Guoguang, Wang Luolin and Li Jingwen. Beijing: Shehui kexue wenxian chubanshe, 1999–.

In the effort to gain a stronger position within the country, and better recognition outside China, the academy also began in 1998 to appoint foreign scholars as Honorary Researchers, equivalent to Honorary Fellows, who are expected to improve its profile. A recent study of CASS traces the changing role of the academy since its separation from the Academy of Science; Margaret Sleeboom, *Academic nationalism* (In English, with

Chinese title, *Xueshu minzuzhuyi*). *Vol. 1. Its categorizations and consequences explored in China and Japan; Vol. 2. Institutional role of CASS in the formation of the Chinese nation-state*. Leiden: International Institute for Asian Studies, Leiden University, 2001.

The reforms in the Academia Sinica in Taipei that have led to the establishment of new discipline-based institutes in the social sciences and humanities have not been easy. The strong determination to reform, however, is guided by a desire to recognise the importance of non-laboratory fields of knowledge that had been organised in unsystematic ways. Specifically, disciplines like sociology, linguistics, philosophy, law and political science have been identified to support the well-established institutes of history, economics and anthropology.

6 The "Three Represents" (*sange daibiao*, representing advanced productive forces, progressive culture, and the interests of all the people) captures this echo of an older holistic political tradition, but it is too early to say if this particular manifestation put forth by Jiang Zemin will prevail. There are almost daily exhortations in the media to study this new principle, suggesting a lack of popular interest. A fairly representative example of this campaign may be found in *Sange daibiao yu lilun chuangxin* (The theoretical originality of the Three Represents), 2001.

7 Waley, "A Debt to China", in *A Harp with a Thousand Strings*, p. 345.

8 Ivan Morris, ed., *Madly Singing*, p. 80, quoted in chapter one. I first met Arthur Waley in 1955 when he gave a public lecture at the School of Oriental and African Studies (SOAS) in London and was tempted to ask him why he never considered visiting China himself. He gave us a hint by telling us the story of calling on the Professor of Chinese at SOAS about studying and translating Chinese poetry. The professor discouraged him by

telling him that there was not much worth doing there. He noted that the professor had come to that conclusion after having lived a long time in a China that had been transformed by the West. The China he himself wanted to study, however, was what was there before "modernity" began to change it beyond recognition.

Perhaps not everyone would agree that Noel Annan has named everyone of importance among the generation that shaped British cultural life after the Second World War, but the irrelevance of China was clear. Of the three men Waley named, Bertrand Russell could not be ignored and Lowes Dickinson earned a few unflattering mentions, but there was no reference to their thoughts on China. Even Waley himself did not appear anywhere. The only exception, not named by Waley, was Harold Acton who did try to capture a bit of modern Chinese poetry, but he too did so before the Second World War (see note 11 following). Once the link with a supine and helpless China as the victim was broken, there did not seem to have been much reason to talk about the British readiness "to make friends and learn", Noel Annan, *Our Age: the Generation that made Post-War Britain*. London: Weidenfeld and Nicolson, 1990.

9 It is often forgotten that Pearl Buck won the Nobel Prize for Literature in 1938, the first for novels about China, *The Good Earth* (1931), *Sons* (1932), and *A House Divided* (1935) probably being the best known. Her friendship for the Chinese was deep and genuine, and her books about their lives won them much sympathy in the West. At least ten of her novels, mostly written in the 1930s, have never been out of print. No other author writing about China in English can claim a similar popular success.

10 G. Lowes Dickinson, *Letters from John Chinaman*. London: Johnson, 1902, published in New York under a different title, *Letters from a Chinese Official:*

being an eastern view of western civilization. New York: McClure, Phillips, 1903. Ernest Bramah, *Kai Lung Unrolls his Mat.* London: Richards Press, 1928, was preceded by *The Wallet of Kai Lung.* London: Methuen, 1917 and *Kai Lung's Golden Hours.* London: Richards, 1922.

11 Harold Acton translated poetry with Ch'en Shih-hsiang, *Modern Chinese Poetry.* London: Duckworth, 1936; and stories with Li Yi-hsieh, *Four Cautionary Tales* (from a collection edited in 1672 by Feng Meng-lung). New York: Wyn, 1937; followed by his novel, *Peonies and Ponies.* London: Chatto and Windus, 1941.

Index